Passing

by

G. A. A. Kent

To my Special friend Phil,

from Gody x

Passing Clouds

© G. A. A. Kent

Published by Bronwyn Editions in the UK 2019

http://www.bronwynbooks.co.uk

Cover design by David Hayes

ISBN: 9781796744453

Dedication

This book is dedicated to all kids growing up in the 1940's wherever they were.

Acknowledgements

To Bernadette Morris: a long-standing special friend who sparked the idea that I should have a go at writing my own story.

I also pay homage to my long-suffering old buddy, Bob Clarke, for all the help and encouragement he gives to me.
Without these two people it would not have worked.

1

I was born at a place called Draycott House, Draycott, Derbyshire, on Sunday March 7th, 1937. This was Mothering Sunday, much to the delight of my mum and the disapproval of my 6-year-old sister, Alma.

My birth certificate was issued on May 3rd 1937 in the registration district of Spondon in the County of Derby. This is one of the few official documents that I still have and is now dog-eared and yellow with age. It was stamped with a King George penny stamp.

I think my infancy was happy and secure. I had a big posh pram and I was spoiled.

One of my first clear memories was being given a big red wooden train for my birthday, or it may have been for Christmas. I kept it for years before it went to my younger cousin, Billy.

We lived at No 2, Dale Street, Burton-upon-Trent, Staffs. It was a rented terraced house which had three bedrooms upstairs and front room, back room and kitchen downstairs. There was an outside toilet, coalhouse, a small yard and garden with a shed at the end. This is the only house I remember where we lived until I was a teenager.

My dad was a lorry driver called Thomas Albert Kent. My mother called him Albert (as did close family) but his workmates called him Tom. My sister and I just knew him as Dad.

He was a tall, handsome man, quiet and shy. He never spoke unless he had something to say and I never, ever heard him swear. For all that he was a man's man.

He wasn't nosey, was always respectful to people and would always help out. He was also the most honest and hardworking man I ever knew.

The story goes that he was raised in Coton-in-the-Elms, Staffs with his parents, younger brother and sister. They had a smallholding and their own piece of land and were quite well off. My father had his own pony and doves.

My grandfather, also called Tom, had the contract for the local pit (coal mine) to break through the face which is what they called when opening up new areas to work the coal. He had his own crew for this and they would put in the props and beams to form the access tunnel for the men and railway track.

He was a big strong man and used to hold up the beams with his head, until one day he had a brain haemorrhage and died. His wife, my grandmother, died soon after and so the three children were left alone.

My dad was only sixteen years old with a younger brother and sister. Dad managed to get his brother, Billy and sister, Mabel, fixed up with separate relatives. Their property was sold off. My mother told me that when the sale was going on, Dad was working the tractor in the field next to it and could hear it and see all their stuff being taken away. It must have broken his heart.

My father agreed that all monies should be put in trust for the keep of his two siblings and that he would be okay as he had some work with the farmer and others.

I don't know what happened with the little ones. I think Mabel was okay, but my uncle Bill used to have to sign a book every week to release his money until it had all gone. He had to eat in the kitchen because he was left-handed. He grew up to be a fine man, a good husband and a great dad. He had an exceptional military career and was a World War 2 veteran. At the end of his career he was an RSM in the Royal Artillery. He was ambidextrous so able to use both hands equally.

Auntie Mabel grew up and married a nice chap; I knew him as Uncle Arthur. He worked as a foreman in the potteries at Stoke-on-Trent. They had two children.

My dad was now alone and I think there was a slump on because I heard he found a job as a dustman. There was a bunch of blokes after this job, so the boss told them to take their jackets off. My dad was a big lad for his age and the boss said, 'You look ready for work with your sleeves rolled up, you can start now.'

I've heard this story before but in my dad's case I believe it was true.

In the end he joined the army, lying about his age. According to the Army records he was two years older than his real age. That must have been his only lie because I never knew him to lie or swear. I suppose this was the time that my dad left Coton-in-the-Elms and I suppose he would have been seeing my mum. She also originated from Coton and I know they both went to the same school.

Dad always had at least one bandage on somewhere (usually his knees) as he was always falling out of trees or into the village pond. I used to love their childhood stories and my sister and I used to encourage them to tell us repeatedly at Sunday dinner times when we always sat together round the table. In fact, our meals were always at the table: breakfast, dinner, tea and sometimes lunch, high tea, supper and never a loaf of bread or milk bottle or drinking vessel without a saucer.

My mother was named Ethel May Skivington. Her father, Arthur, worked at the coal mine.

Their children were: Florence

Tom

Ethel (Mum)

Phil

Evelyn (uncle Bill's wife)

Charlie

My grandad and grandma Skivington moved to Burton it seemed, and the rest must have followed because by the time I became aware everyone was posted in and around Burton.

2, Dale Street was my home until I was fourteen years old, where I saw through World War 2 and some. I am almost ashamed to say that I had a lovely war and a very happy childhood, full of fun, friends and family. We were a large close family with aunties, uncles and loads of cousins.

Our next door neighbours and landlords were called Jack and Ivy Leedham. They had a son, John, who was about the same age as my sister. We always got on with them very well. They were cattle merchants and they were at No 1 Dale Street.

Between our two houses there was a pair of large green doors, fitted with a wicket door for easy access. This led into a big entry, above which there were two bedrooms; the front one was part of the Leedham's house and the rear one was ours.

The entry led out onto a large yard with outbuildings at the end. Most of the time these were occupied by pigs.

After my big red train, my next memories were of laughing a lot at a very silly Mam. She used to sing to me, make silly noises and talk to me in comical voices. The more I laughed, the worse she got!

A few years later, when *The Goon Show* started, I thought my Mam could have been in it. I loved that show; it was so stupid and witty for its time. I also picked the humour up, because animals love it when you behave silly with them. It's as if they can sense you are happy. I think this is why a lot of people love their pets because they can't tell the rest of the world just how daft their owner really is.

I think my Dad was away in the army. He joined the Royal Horse Artillery, as in those days a lot of guns were still horse-drawn and my Dad knew a bit about those animals. There was always an old framed photo of him on the wall, with him sitting at an occasional table in uniform. The uniform was shorts, leggings (I think they were called putties), boots with spurs and a short-sleeved shirt. He was holding a horse whip and on the small table was his hat, a round safari hat, also known as a pith helmet.

I think he was in India, way before Mahatma Ghandi, when Britain ruled India.

My next early memory is that I had been promoted from my lovely bouncy posh pram into a push chair, from which I managed to escape several times.

Once my sister took me to a place called the Ox Hay, a large playing field and area over the Trent bridge. She linked up with some of her mates and then went home without me. Mum said, 'Where's your baby brother?' and Alma replied, 'Oh, I forgot him.'

Someone went and collected me; I was still sitting in my chair, fast asleep, on the pathway next to the river. I don't remember any of this, but I was told about it later.

I jokingly said to Alma, 'You left me on purpose,', but I know she always hated having to look after me and cart me around. She told me many times that she wanted to be an only child.

Another push chair story was the night we came home from a party. It was about midnight, dark and bitterly cold. I think it was a Christmas party of relatives and we had to walk home from an area called Hornington, about two miles from home. I was in my push chair and I think all the grown-ups were warmed up with Burton beer. I remember how cold my bare legs were and also my feet. I always wore short trousers. I was so tired and too cold to sleep. I remember thinking how nice it would be to be back in my pram. It seemed a long way home; and that's the last time I remember being in a pushchair.

The next big thing in my life, after my red train, was a dog called Bonzo. He was big and black. I think he was a Labrador. Apparently Mum had agreed to look after him for a while for this young couple. I didn't hear all that. He was mine to ride, pull around, poke him and pull his ears. If he was not following me around, then I was following him. I loved him; he even used to sleep in my room.

Then one day the couple returned to collect him and take him back with them to live in Chesterfield. They seemed a nice couple and

Bonzo liked them a lot. It didn't help, but they promised to bring him back to see me, which they did a couple of times. He always remembered me, although I was very upset for a couple of days. I also knew and was told that they would return to take him home one day. I learned very early on that love and possession are not the same thing.

It was lovely to see him again when he came to visit. I realised at a later time that the couple came to see my mother and brought the dog with them for my benefit, which was thoughtful of them.

People were like that back then. I still loved Bonzo, my first of many animals.

I suppose the war was on by now. I was allowed to play out in the back garden which was long and narrow. It had a three-foot paling fence and a small entrance gate from Leedham's yard, as it was called. We had a long path leading up to my Dad's shed with a strip of garden on the left side, next to the fence with a lilac tree. On the right was an outbuilding extension from the house which contained the kitchen, with an entrance door, an outhouse, a coalhouse and the outside toilet.

After the outbuilding, there was a small open area of hardstanding. I remember a big stone slab shelf, two rabbit hutches and beyond them a chicken run. So, whilst my Dad was away sorting out that Hitler bloke almost single-handedly (with some help from Errol Flynn and John Wayne), the garden was mine as long as I kept clear of Mum's rose bush, rhubarb and mint.

I would play for hours building mud pies, castles, trenches, worm tasting, fly killing and generally getting as dirty as possible. My mother was great fun but my sister was disgusted with me. I never used to see a lot of her as she was always keeping low in case she had to take me somewhere or look after me.

During this time, I fell in love with the second dog in my life. His name was Beauty. He was called Beauty because he was the ugliest bull mastiff you ever saw. I don't remember how it came about, but I remember he was usually chained up in Leedham's yard. I used to look at him through the palings of the fence.

He had a big kennel and he was a guard dog. We soon became friends and we had limited space in common. His chain would reach up to our fence and he used to come over to see me. I could reach him with my arm to pat him and tickle his tummy. Once the Leedhams and my Mum saw how well we got on, I was allowed to go into the yard. I would sit with Beauty for hours and would pull him around just like I had done with Bonzo. Beauty was a big softy and he loved to watch me colouring in my books, adding his slobber to the odd page and chewing the odd crayon. He preferred chalk though, but it was banned after I coloured his nose and nails in blue, my favourite colour. We brightened up his kennel with coloured chalk and, as I grew up, I never ignored him. We would always greet each other when I came home from school.

Between this period and starting infant school I became aware that there was a war on. Mam and I used to see a lot of people and every Saturday we would go to my Grandad and Grandma's house, where the whole family would meet up. The men would go to the pub for a couple of hours and the women would chatter and catch up with their gossip. The men would return, usually happy and noisy, and then sometimes my Grandad would play his violin.

He was a superb violinist, better than good. He used to play a lot of classical music and he could sight-read music, i.e. play a new piece straight from the sheet.

They tried to get him on the radio, but he was too shy. He would bring up the hairs on my neck and I realised that I loved good music. I so enjoyed these evenings. We were such a loving, big, loyal family.

These meetings continued throughout the War but all the men disappeared to go to war, except for Grandad. They would be there if they were on leave, which was good, as I enjoyed all their war stories.

My sister would take me out sometimes with her round to her mates. Sometimes we had good fun. Most of her mates liked having me around and liked looking after me. This made it easier for Alma if they didn't mind her kid brother tagging along. They used to think that I spoke nicely and this was because of my mother. As I was learning to speak, my Mam used to pick me up on proper pronunciation, using the whole of a word and no slang words. Swearing was only for "very common and lowly people". "People who swear never learn to speak properly". I think she was probably right, but she was such a snob with it.

I had various illnesses, including chickenpox, and my tonsils out around this time.

2

Following my illnesses, I was left with double vision. When I wanted to focus I had to strain my left eye into the inner corner to make my vision clear. I had to be fitted with spectacles and I wore an obscure white lens over the left eye for a while. I had to wear glasses until I was twenty years old, which I hated, especially as I had become a very physically active kid. This was considering that the doctor had warned my mother not to be surprised if I couldn't keep up with the others, as I could be a bit sickly and weaker following my illnesses.

So, I was not a pretty child. My blond curls had gone. I had straight mousy hair that always stood up and was all over the place, a wonky eye and a pair of round wire glasses that were also wonky, held together with adhesive tape. I was not a "poser", I left that to my sister, but I was always happy.

I must have been about four years old now. It was 1941. I liked listening to the "wireless" (radio), especially music, most of which was classical and light music. Ballads and Jazz were just beginning. My first favourite song was *Somewhere Over the Rainbow* by Judy Garland.

There was plenty going on in and around the town. With the War Effort there used to be parties and dances, travelling circuses, fairs, cinemas and the like to cheer people up.

There weren't many men about. "Our boys are away fighting" the women used to say. Things went onto rationing and everyone was given a gas mask. Mine was a pink one called a Mickey Mouse mask.

Occasionally we would get free food supplies from the government, which would be a box containing dried milk, coffee, flour and other items.

Everyone used to knit or darn socks, mend or make clothes and save wool and rags, as everything was in short supply. It was wonderful the way we all pulled together; everyone was nice to each other.

Sometimes I was allowed to sit on the front step of our house after it was dry. All front steps were usually scrubbed in the morning by the woman of the house - wearing a house coat, curlers and headscarf seemed to be the norm. I loved to watch the street life - the bread, milk, coal, etc. all by horse and cart. The baker, who was a friend, used to stop at our house for a cuppa as nos 1 and 2 Dale Street were his last drop-offs. He would put a feed bag on his horse whilst he waited. His horse nearly always did a poo and we would take out a bucket and shovel and take it through to the back garden for the rose bush and the rhubarb.

Bread was always a proper loaf; there was no sliced bread then, or wrappings, or gloves. Sometimes, if you were lucky, you would cut a slice of bread to find you had cut right through a dead spider. Apparently, after turning off the ovens, spiders used to crawl inside to keep warm, get locked in with the next day's baking and burrow into the soft yeast to try and escape the heat and then get baked. My mam said that it was quite common, as indeed it was, as it happened a couple of times after. I told the baker and he gave me a free bun. About four years later I was on my way to school and he shouted across the road 'Had any spiders lately?' I said 'Yes, two.'

He gave me a paper bag with some buns in it and said with a grin, 'Take them to school and share with your friends.' He was our bread man for many years even after we moved house. I remember making him a coffee table once, but that is all in the future and I am back in the war years. I remember wanting to cut my own "doorstep". That is what we called a thick slice of bread, but

Mam, that is what I called her then, which was the local twang for mother, said I was too young. I always wanted to get hands-on.

Our milk was delivered straight from the dairy at the end of the street and would come in pint bottles with a wider top than today's and the top would be a round cardboard push in top with a small perforated circle that you would push your finger through in order to pull out the top.

A short time later, during my school days, I used to nip down to the dairy and scrounge a box of new ones from the girls who worked there and take them to school to play flicking with, which was a game we used to play with cigarette cards. In those days, most cigarette packs would come with a card inside with a picture of a famous footballer, or sport star, flower, etc. depending on the brand of cig. And you would try to collect the full set and there always seemed to be more of some pictures than others. Reason I suppose was a sales pitch. Anyhow this made some cards more sought after than others and when swapping, a rare card would be worth more than one back so you would barter a deal. And I used to give out ten milk bottle tops for one cig card in mint condition, because flicking the cards to win other cards by going the farthest or nearest the wall used to knock the corners off and make them dirty, plus when they got dog-eared they did not fly so well. So, trying to be enterprising, I suggested that they used the bottle tops with their mark on the back for the contest after agreeing which cards they were playing for. It caught on well until the headmistress banned them as the kids were all twanging them at each other and they did come a bit sharp when hit in the face, and I suppose they could damage an eye. So we continued to use them in friendly street fights. These were nothing like the street fights to follow.

The coalmen would also deliver by horse and cart. Our normal order would be two bags of coal and one bag of slack. The slack would bank up the fire so it would burn slowly if you needed to pop out, or keep it going through the night, and you always put in place a fireguard as anything that burned would go on the fire, even vegetable peelings. We had open fireplaces in the living room, front room, and two bedrooms. The living room fire place was wrought iron with a wooden mantle and tiled hearth with a large fender and there was a companion set stood in the hearth, holding a small brush, pan, poker, and a toasting fork, and to the left of the hearth was the coal scuttle. We always made toast from the fire, but I wasn't allowed yet.

When the coal and dustmen came, Beauty was put inside the house and the big gates were opened. The coal bags were made of rope, and the dustbins made of mild steel. Dustbins were round with two handles and a round lid with handle in the middle of the top to enable the lid to be lifted on and off the container base, like a hat to keep out the flies, rats, etc. and keep in the bad smells. They were made in a corrugated style for extra strength and mild steel 'cos people used to put hot ashes in them, plus strong plastic wasn't invented yet.

The bins would usually be kept inside an outbuilding like the coal and both the coal and dustbins would normally be carried by one man. The dust cart would also be horse drawn, and I did so enjoy so many horses; they all seemed well fed and well turned out and I think they were happy doing their different jobs. And I must mention those magnificent shire horses that delivered the beer in and around Burton. They would deliver the dray barrels to all the pubs in town. I think there was a pub in every street - they were so well groomed and turned out, wearing highly polished leather and brasses.

They looked so big and majestic as if they knew they were doing dressage on parade.

Most other people, like chimney sweep, builders, etc. would have handcarts, sometimes with their names written on. Cars were quite rare along our street as all useful vehicles had been confiscated for the War Effort. The Leedhams next door had a car and a cattle lorry with a trailer; otherwise it would be doctors or people with special jobs. Even iron railings and gates were taken and melted down to make weapons, etc. although at Christ Church, just around the corner, they did retain their front railings.

The lampposts were cast iron. They remained, but were never lit up during the war, and cars that had to be used at night would have peaks over the top of the headlights and often a slit in a metal lens cover that fitted over the headlight to prevent the beams showing too much, so as not to be seen from the sky. Also all windows had to have a black blind that covered the whole of the glass area so that not a peek of light could be seen from outside. It was usually a black roller blind made of linen or strong paper, and then the curtains drawn over that. These were always checked out every night by the air raid warden.

The lampposts were great fun. We used to love climbing up them and swinging on the bars at the top. They were there to support the small ladder for the lamplighter when lighting and dowsing the lamps, or maintaining, as they were still oil lamps then. Sometimes you would see a lamppost with one and even both of its arms, as we used to call them, broken off, but cast iron will break quite easily if hit in the right place. We had about six in our street.

Most of the road traffic was bicycles: big heavy things a bit like cars really, pretty much same make. Raleigh, made in Nottingham, with black sit-up-and-beg handlebars. Some were delivery bikes with large baskets on the front and some even had a sign-written nameplate under the crossbar. Some with a barrow that fitted on the back, some with three wheels, some with blocks on the pedals, some tandems, but I never did see a penny farthing on our street.

Around this time Mam and I were spending a lot of time together. Alma was at school getting ready for her secondary selection exams. We did a lot of visiting friends and relations. And they all used to say, "Oh, doesn't he speak nicely". That was because my mother would correct my speech all the time and elocution. On leaving school my mother had gone into service - that meant you were employed by a rich family in a big house starting as a maid. This seemed to have impressed my mother for the rest of her life: the way they spoke, dressed, took high tea at 4pm. And how to dine with silver service, etc. and after the war, every Sunday we would all sit around the table together for a roast dinner. And always a home-made pudding, and sometimes we would have a large slice of Yorkshire pudding covered with gravy as a starter. Dad would always carve the meat and Mam would do the rest, and we would always eat off good china, with real silver cutlery, even fish knives and forks, when eating fish dishes. Even the vegetables would be in china vegetable dishes with lids to match and large silver serving spoons. Most of this stuff was given to her by her employer when she left service, including a crown Derby set. Yes, she had the lot. She was such a snob and yet the best Mam. All through the war my sister and I never went hungry or really wanted for anything.

We kept our food inside a small storage room at the end of the kitchen, which had a doorway, small window on the outer wall that opened and a large square air brick underneath the window. It was as long as the kitchen width and approx. four feet wide. We called it the scullery, or pantry, or larder. Inside it had storage shelves for food, tins, also hooks for hanging veg, game, etc. a large marble slab from wall to wall under the window and, on the right-hand side, we had a cupboard made of wood with a middle shelf and fitted with a side hung panelled door. The door panel was made of a metal sheet with fine perforated holes through it and so called a mesh - to allow air flow, and inside this we would keep cheese, butter, milk, cold meat and all the things one would keep inside a fridge today, as we did not have refrigerators in those days. We called it the meat safe.

Also in the scullery, we would keep our outdoor clothing: footwear, shoe brushes, polish and house cleaning stuff and, on the floor behind the door would be the mangle that was brought out on washday, along with the dolly tub that was half of a beer barrel and made the same way. In fact, in Burton, it probably was a beer barrel cut in half to make two dolly tubs. With that was the dolly or washing peg. This was a tool made of wood and looked a bit like a milkmaid's stool and, let into the middle of the top, would be a round peg a bit like a long rolling pin. Then towards the top there it would have another peg like a dowel going right through the main stem upright. So it looked a bit like a lamppost and the arms at the top were your handlebars and each side would be long enough for a big hand. And this was called your dolly. It stood about three feet. in height and what you would do, usually the lady of the house, was put soapy water into the dolly tub, chuck in some dirty clothes, put in dolly, swish it around one way then the other, a bit like driving a bus out of control. Some dollies were fitted with a rubber plunger type base instead of the pegs. Also there was a washboard for extra dirty items and spots made of beechwood or wood and metal and used mostly on small items, a big block of soap and scrubbed over the dolly tub. Then rinse all thoroughly, put through the mangle, (mind your fingers) then hang out to dry. Empty dirty water, tip down the drain and clean yard if outside. Otherwise bale out water from dolly tub into sink with saucepan, put all away and tidy up kitchen.

Go down to the gym for a workout whilst the clothes are drying. Ready for the evening's ironing whilst listening to wireless after tea.

By the way, there was also a carpet beater round the back of the scullery door made of cane. But I don't think I will go there.

3

Another item that was kept in the end room was Mam's laundry basket. It was round with two handles and made of willow, made by blind people. Mam used to buy her shopping baskets and wooden clothes pegs from them also. And hanging on the wall would be an oval long tin bath with a handle at each end and was galvanized so as not to rust. These tin baths are still being made today, as they are in great demand for garden planters, builders for mixing compounds, etc.

Other items I can remember are outdoor clothing: hats, shoes, wellie boots, shoe polish and brushes and many other handy items for the running of a home.

Mam was good at organising stuff, probably learned from working in service. We always kept candles in there; more than four, ha-ha. We used to get a lot of power cuts what with the war going on, and electricity was in its early days.

Indeed, our electricity then would be condemned today. It consisted of a 2-core cable, i.e. two copper wires sheathed in silk cord and twisted together, and would be face-fixed to skirting boards, door frames, walls, and ceilings by a small staple at intervals. The staples had a small leather sleeve on the upper inside to protect the wires from making direct contact with each other. Then it would go from junction to junction which, in our home, would be a single two pin plug socket in all downstairs rooms and a ceiling light fitting to all others, including bedrooms. The wall plugs, ceiling roses and light fitting holders, inside which the wire connections were made, were of a very hard material called *Bakelite* which was used for many products during the war years, including radio cases, parts of telephones and a thousand other things. It was the forerunner of the development of plastic. The electric cables came from our supply meter that was in the kitchen.

In fact, in our home we still had gas lights on all the main walls. These consisted of a gas pipe on or coming through the wall, bent upwards with a gas mantel and a small shade that fitted on the top. The mantels would burn out after a while and you would replace them with new ones that could be purchased from any hardware shop. Each light would have a thumb and finger turn valve button to allow the gas to be on or off and adjust the pressure to work like a dimmer switch. The streetlights would work the same way. I don't know whether ours were in working order or not. I suspect they were as we had a gas cooker and a gas Ascot water heater in the kitchen with a long spout over the old-fashioned, butler stone-enamelled sink. Why would my mother bother about wallpapering around them and keeping them clean otherwise, but I don't remember ever seeing them.

The entrance to the larder was a plain ledged and braced door, same as the outside toilet, coal house, and outhouse, i.e. made of pine wood and was tongue and grooved boarding held together by nailing them onto three wooden straps called top middle and bottom rails. These would be fastened together with a nail that would go in from the face side boarding, right through the rails and then clenched over into the backside rails; then a couple of rails about four inches by one inch would be cut and fixed in the same way, between the rails, to form brackets as in gallows brackets. These would be 'handed' as the bracket should always go up from the hinged side and never be cut at less than 45°.

This was the cheapest door in those days except for a ledged type. These were good serviceable doors and many of them are still swinging away to this day. Anyway, our larder door opened inwards by putting your finger through a hole and lifting up the iron latch, which was also always tight and stiff because the frame and door were a bit twisted. When one lifted the latch it would echo from the pantry and kitchen all over the house and got me into some minor trouble a couple of years later when stealing some cheese for my pet mouse, Timothy, during the night.

Another item that springs to mind, as hanging on the back of this door was a spare back door key, and it was a massive old-fashioned iron rim lock key. It was so big and heavy you could not lose it and I don't think we used it anyway - people didn't lock their back doors much in those days plus, to get into our back door, you would have to get past Beauty, after getting through the big gates or climbing over a brick wall with broken glass bedded into a cement fillet on the top. The only time our back door was locked was when I was older and Alma had to look after me on a Saturday whilst Mam was at work, and that was bolted on the inside when I was out playing and she wouldn't let me back in.

The scullery/pantry/larder had a small opening fanlight window. All the other windows were the lovely old wooden sliding up and down sash windows with cords and lead weights. When I was a bit older, I used to marvel at the way they worked; so ingenious but simple, little realising that one day soon I would be able to make one with ease, and if made and painted properly, you could just feel a trickle of air coming through the sides, which was good for the wood and the rooms. All the internal doors were wooden four-panelled, i.e. top rail, middle rail, bottom rail, two middle upright rails called mullions and two outside rails called styles, and these would all be grooved on the inside face edges to let in the four panels that were also made of solid pine wood, as plywood was only good enough for tea chests and the like in those days.

All these parts would be fitted together with mortice and tenon joints and glued together with hot glue or wood priming paint. The front and back doors were made on the same principle except they were thicker, and the back door had glass at the top half and the front door had moulded panels. Hot glue would not be used on the external doors; in those days tenons would go all the way through the styles with wooden wedges driven in the gaps so as to form a dovetail joint, making it harder to come apart.

External glue was not really available yet. Although these old doors were commonplace then, they were well made and, if not abused, would last indefinitely.

These old doors are still sought after and in great demand today. The wooden door frames had a moulded architrave both sides, upstairs and down the pattern of the architrave is called "ogee". It was also on the picture rail that ran around the same rooms, as well as top of the skirting boards which were deeper than today's standard skirting at about nine inches deep.

The staircase was also made of pine - quite narrow with a mopstick handrail on the left side going up; these were very steep. To go upstairs you would open the bottom door outwards, hinged on the left and would open onto the chimney recess wall to reveal a one step landing, then proceed up the stairs to the top landing called a "well" as there was a one step up to the first floor, i.e. bedroom floor levels.

The left front bedroom (mine), right back bedroom (Mam and Dad), straight ahead (Alma's room). Coming down was always tricky especially if you were carrying something like a tray or a chamber pot with a Number one or Number two in it and the bottom door might be closed. Trouble was that the stair treads were never big enough in these old houses due to not having the distance called "going" to allow more treads, but this was standard practice in the day to save space and land (some things don't change). They would not pass building regulations today and I never met anyone who didn't slip or fall down them at some time. In fact, in my Uncle Tom's terraced house, was a quarter turn at the bottom of his stairs which was three treads cut on an angle called fans and built in so that the three bottom steps went from nothing to really stand on at the inside to quite a bit on the outside. This was okay when you got used to them, but not a good idea at the bottom of some very steep stairs, plus a door to deal with. And my Uncle Tom was always pissed.

Other fixtures in our home were four open fireplaces, i.e. front room, living room and the two main bedrooms that would take up the same area as the downstairs rooms below, as the smaller rear bedroom was situated above the large entry and it had no heating. In fact, those four open fireplaces were our only source of heating in those days and the bedroom fires were only used if someone was poorly, or if it was really cold and we had a good stock of coal. I was quite poorly a couple of times during these years and I remember how I loved the coal fire burning and making the bedroom feel cosy and didn't mind the light not being on because the fire would light up the room enough and I would watch it ember into the night and the patterns flickering on the wall and ceiling until I went to sleep. I still get transfixed when I see an open fire burning, whether it be log or coal, and I don't think I am alone on that one as I can remember many times sitting round a pub fire on a freezing cold night and having a pint more than I needed because my mates and I were enjoying the moment.

I liked my bedroom; it was a good size and had a large cupboard over the stair bulkhead, and Alma preferred the small room overlooking the big back yard, plus my bedroom window overlooked the street which could get very noisy, especially at night, and weekends at pub closing time. You could always hear blokes talking loudly and worse. But I didn't mind all that and, when I got tired after being out playing, nothing would keep me awake, plus I enjoyed the hustle and bustle of the street. But people used to like to lie in on a Sunday and the back of the houses were usually quieter, except for Tweedle-Dum; he was our rooster who lived in the chicken pen at the end of our garden, and nobody told him about Sunday, so he decided that everyone should be awake by 5 a.m. and took it upon himself to do reveille every morning. He was a massive bird and I used to tease him rotten, but I paid the price later in my story.

Mam would always open up the front room on Sundays and if cold would light a fire; otherwise the room would feel damp and smell musty and the three-piece suite would feel damp when sat on. People used to peep through the window sometimes when passing because we had a large good carpet on top of fitted lino, a big three-piece suite, occasional table, glass fronted display cabinet, upright piano, all highly French polished, real oil paintings on the wall, etc. Mam and Alma loved it, but I didn't, especially when I started going out to play and the other kids used to say, "Oh you live in that posh house with the big dog, don't you?"

I used to hate Sundays. Always had to wear my Sunday clothes, was not allowed to play properly and had to go for long walks in the afternoon with the grown-ups, i.e. Aunties and Uncles, plus listen to them all chattering and whispering, and not realising what a lucky little sod I was.

Before I finish with the home comforts, it did get very cold at nights during the winter months and one would awaken with a cold wet nose and then have to get out of bed and dress. Later, when I was at school and had to get myself up and dressed, I used to count up to ten, then jump out of bed and go for it, and there was usually a long pause between numbers nine and ten. Then I started laying my underpants, vest and socks on the sideboard next to my bed for easy reach and removing my pyjamas whilst still in bed, and then get up, followed by reaching over to grab these items off the sideboard without getting out of bed, thus taking the chill off the cold underwear before removing my pyjamas so I would end up with my underclothes on by the time I got out of bed. This routine went on for a short while until I got into a ravel one morning and, whilst searching for my clean underpants, as I lifted back the bed cover they fell from underneath it straight into the chamber pot which I had not pushed far enough under the bed. After that I decided to brave the cold, and we always had warm beds and wrapped up well outside - plus it is good that your body learns to cope with some cold temperatures, and good fresh air was never in short supply.

The only places with central heating back then were large houses and public buildings like schools and hospitals. These required a large gas or coal boiler, and big heavy cast-iron radiators. We all had hot water bottles at bedtime; electric blankets were not around either, heavy thick curtains over windows and often doors to stop the draft and for blackout. We also used to make draught stoppers for the bottom of doors. Some people would knit them like a snake and fill them with a weighty material and sometimes pushed the stuffing into a stocking and laid along the bottom of a door.

The kitchen never seemed to be a problem for heating, as we had a gas cooker that was used every day for something - even the whistling kettle against the internal wall. On the opposite external wall, on the left of the sink above a beech wooden draining board that ran down and into the sink, was the Ascot water heater with an ongoing pilot light, and on the left, filling the gap between the sink and the pantry wall was a brick built copper water heater. This was our main hot water supply for Monday washing, bathing, household cleaning, etc. Mam used to boil whites in it like bed sheets, shirts, hankies, nappies and anything that was grimed.

This was a simple construction and worked very well. It was made by building a brick housing unit on a firm solid non-flammable base. Ours was on stone flags - and the brickwork was built in order to place the copper bowl into the top and had to be a good fit so as not to allow smoke to come out of the lip of the copper top from the fire underneath. When in use, the fire was lit and cleaned out with access via a small iron door that was hinged to a metal frame and had a latch on one side to keep it closed. This was built into the brickwork. A second one was built in a bit higher and to the left and was used for stoking up and adding fuel. I suppose these iron doors would have been a standard item in those days and purchased from a merchant. There were many foundries then.

These doors were about six inches square. The top was flat with a large hole cut into it to sit the copper bowl into and there would have been another hole at the inner corner between the outside kitchen wall and the scullery wall because there was a small brick chimney going up into the corner and through the kitchen ground floor roof. I think the boiler top was quarry tiles onto stone slab. It may have been concrete, but I think not, as concrete had not been reinvented when the house was built. The height of the top from ground level was about three feet. The lid was a big round wooden one made the same way as the doors of the outbuildings i.e. one-inch boarding held together with two wooden straps and with a large wooden handle. A few years later, after the war, my Dad made a new one and the old one was chucked at the end of the garden. I thought it looked like an old Vikings' shield and I used it when Dale Street had a stone fight with Canal Street.

When I was small, I would sometimes get my bath in the copper; then later, I would sit on the copper with my feet in the big enamel kitchen sink and have a wash down, especially if I had been out playing, as I always had dirty feet, and it was quick and easy, and when I was young I wasn't very interested in keeping clean.

When I look back, I appreciate all the great simple but clever ideas that really worked, like this household boiler, and how hard the people worked to hold things together, especially during the war, and the spirit and the backbone of ordinary people who I grew up with and it was instilled in me from my first learning what a great little nation we were, all in all.

The kitchen walls were painted to a gloss finish onto the brickwork, as was the scullery, and the ceilings were all painted with distemper whitewash including the frieze, that is the part between the ceiling and picture rail. We used to get our whitewash from Jack Leedham (Mr to me), our landlord, as he was always painting out his pigsties and sheds each time he got in new livestock. So he always had loads. And emulsion paint was not invented yet. That was another problem; if you had an accident like accidentally kicking the jerry (chamber pot) over, upstairs, it would pour straight between the floorboards onto the ceiling below because the flooring was wooden boards butted together, without a tongue and groove in those days, and you would be left with an embarrassing stain on your ceiling - another good reason to have lino with a good overlap in the bedrooms.

Mam had wallpapered all of the plastered walls including the stairway and landing. Wallpaper was not very exciting in those days and always looked a bit dowdy to me with only two or three colours and it used to come with a border each side about half an inch wide. This would be a plain paper strip, but part of the wallpaper and would be perforated like a postage stamp along the line where the pattern started and, depending on which way you were working, you would take off the border from the side of the new piece going on so that it would overlap the border of the last piece already stuck on the wall, leaving the remaining border on the open side ready to be overlapped by the next piece. The side you wanted to remove would be done by holding the new roll at an angle and tapping it on the corner edge and turning it slowly and it would come off surprisingly easy. Mam used to let me do this job. And the wallpaper paste was plain flour and water. A distemper brush, pair of scissors, clean cloth, kitchen chair, and my Mam did a great job. No level, no plumb bob; she used to start on a door frame trusting it to be plumb, which I suppose was fair enough.

4

We were now late in the year of 1941 and, although we won the battle of Britain, the war was raging on especially in Europe: big ships getting sunk and put out of action on both sides, gaining ground and losing ground, struggling against the onslaught of Rommel's tanks against our Desert Rats, with great loss of lives to both sides. Along the way, Burton had its share of bombs for a small town - more than 200. Although Burton was mostly a brewery town, the breweries were massive and from the air would look like large factories. Most of our industries were in the Midlands and we were only ten miles from Derby (Rolls Royce) and Birmingham. It was reported that Burton got bombed twice being mistaken for Leicester, and I don't suppose the German pilots would have much time to sit around once inland as our ack-ack gunners were well trained and barrage balloons were everywhere, plus their fuel would be getting used up, so they would want to offload all their bombs and get out. The sirens would always go off when they were coming over because we had radar so we always had some time to prepare and most times in Burton we wouldn't get anything until the all clear and we would just carry on with our lives, with the true grit of a Brit. And, joking aside, as a kid we learned how to stand up to big bullies by watching the grown-ups cope and handle things during the war. As a kid you just don't like your enemy who wants to kill you and yours because they are nasty; you're not old enough to know any more than that.

During an air raid we would sometimes go to an air raid shelter that was built on a piece of waste ground we used to call Meller's garden, as a family called Meller lived at the end of it. It was a standard shelter, brick built with a flat concrete roof and inside were two long fixed slatted bench seats where, during a raid, people would fill it with smoke and sing their heads off to Al Jolson, Flanagan and Allen, Vera Lynn, etc. and there was usually someone drunk. I don't remember a street in Burton without a pub. Ha-ha, but it was all in good spirit. Sometimes we would go just around the corner to Christ Church where there were shelters dug into the ground with a mound of turfs on the top so as not to be visible from above; yet most people would go into the church hall, and they would be part of the congregation who wanted to be together, and probably felt safer in church, (I don't suppose any pilot would intentionally bomb a church but most raids were at night.) Most times we would stay home in the scullery, under the table, or if we could hear the planes we would get under the stairs and sit huddled around the gas meter where the main gas supply comes into the house. Ha, although I didn't realise at the time, I would probably have been safer standing in the middle of an open field waving a Union Jack. There is an old saying: *ignorance is bliss.*

Winter time, damp and cold, but homely food was in short supply and just about everything was on ration. Every person was supplied with a ration book that contained tickets that had to be cut out and retained by the shopkeeper when purchasing anything that was on ration, like some foods, clothing, petrol, sweets, etc. People seemed to queue up for everything. Sometimes you would see a queue of people outside a shop before it was open in case they had taken a delivery overnight, which would not have been unusual, but you had to do these things to survive.

Farmers were going flat out to try and keep up with the food demand. Our merchant ships were getting hit, running the gauntlet to cross the English Channel without getting torpedoed by German ships and U-boats. Thank goodness Alma and I had our Mam. She used to terrorise the neighbourhood to get what she needed for her two spoilt brats. I am sure they modelled the Ena Sharples character of *Coronation Street* on her; she was a real "Taurus" but was a good woman and would help anyone in real need. Even the butcher would have Mam's piece of meat put by and Alma would collect it on a Saturday morning without joining the queue. We always seemed to have a nice cut of meat on a Sunday for our silver service dinner; perhaps because of living next door to the local cattle merchants who were our friends and landlords, or because of Uncle Tom who was a local butcher before and after the war, but was a Desert Rat at this time. He was Mam's eldest brother and, though I was very young at this time, I can remember so many observations to appreciate what it was like for the grown-ups. Though they were fighting tooth and nail for their own, the sharing of food and clothes between people, the most basic things in life, made me love and hate the human race, all at the same time.

We were now on the run up to Christmas and just into December when on the 7th the radio announced that the Japanese had attacked the American naval port at Pearl Harbour with an air onslaught causing massive loss of life and damage to the fleet. And that the US had responded by declaring war on Japan, which in turn gave the green light to join ranks with the UK fighting in Europe. Winney would be pleased.

I don't remember anything specific about Christmas but it would have been great as always; there would have been a nice Christmas tree with the same beautiful trinkets on it, new crackers, sometimes home-made, streamers, large paper bells and baubles.

Usually the paper streamers would go from the centre of the ceiling rose to the top of the picture rail and you would not be able to see the living room ceiling for twelve days. On Christmas morning there would be a nice big present under the tree, and a pillowcase full of presents at the end of the bed when we woke up, put there by Santa in the night whilst we were sleeping. He would also leave a Christmas stocking full of nuts and fruit hanging from the mantelpiece. How I loved all these things, but I also knew how lucky I was, and was taught how to appreciate things and people. I had a lot of children's books and clothes that year. I suppose Mam was trying to prepare me for school.

5

Winters in the Midlands were bitterly cold during the war years. I can remember getting into my pyjamas in front of the living room fire; then legging it up the stairs into a freezing cold bedroom and shivering until I warmed up in the lovely warm bed. Sometimes Mam would put in a hot water bottle that was made of clay and glazed on the outside and had a turn screw top with a rubber gasket collar on it to stop it leaking. It was like the one on a jerry can, and this would be situated in the middle of the rounded top. They were made at the nearby potteries at Stoke on Trent and issued free at two per family by the War Supply Department. They were collected from a local hardware shop with the necessary coupon and waiting your turn in the queue, of course. I can remember going to collect them with Mam and Alma and how heavy they were to carry home, and that was when empty, but you didn't miss out on anything that was free during the war, ha-ha. Everything had a use and I bet they would be a collector's item today, like the old stone ginger bottle with a cork or a flip top on it, made the same way, or what a great flower vase or rockery piece.

Anyway, back to bedtime. Sometimes Mam would put a house brick on top of the fire grate hot plate, then wrap it up in a tea towel and put it in the bottom of the bed before bedtime. That was great as you could kick it out during the night without worrying about it breaking or spilling, and it was not in line with the gusunder. We actually also had a warming pan hanging on the wall in the living room, but that was part of Mam's copper and brass collection. It was always highly polished and had a long, wood-turned handle in French polished oak. It looked like a big frying pan to me, and I dread to think of the dangers of placing it in a bed containing hot cinders from the fire.

So, once in bed it wouldn't be long before I would be fast asleep, and the next thing it was morning, and the only thing above the bedding was my head from the nose upwards and this nose was wet and cold. I could see the ice on the inside of the window glass, so I would put my head under the sheets to breathe in the warm stale air rather than the cold fresh air that stung the inside of my nose and made my eyes water.

Then Mam would shout up, 'Come on down, the fire is on.' So that was that. I would shout back, 'Coming Mam!' Although I was spoiled, I only got told once and always answered when expected, and I didn't mind really because she would always cheer me up and make me laugh. She was good in the morning; she just knew how to stand up and face the world for a new day, and it was infectious and stayed with me for the rest of my life, as I was to be well tested in days ahead.

I don't remember if my Dad was on leave or not that Christmas. I know he had a couple of Christmas holidays with us when I was very young and remember blowing bubbles with one of my presents when we were all in Mam and Dads' bed on Christmas morning, opening presents. Then he sang the song "I'm forever blowing bubbles". I had never heard him ever sing before or since and we all fell about laughing, including him (no wonder they promoted him to be in charge of the church organ pump when he tried to join the Coton-in-the-Elms boys' choir). The incident stays in my mind so vividly because he was a shy, strong, silent man. I think he always loved playing with my toys because he never had any himself, and that is another thing about my Dad: I never, ever saw him resentful toward anyone who had something more than him or a better car than him, or anything else.

6

With Christmas and New Year, which were great as usual, behind us, we were now into 1942. The war raged on and now the Americans had entered; it was a world war as there was not a country that was not affected by it in one way or another. And the American intervention boosted the morale of the Brits and Churchill; America supplied us with nearly 1,000 tanks and other weapons, ammo, and hardware, and started setting up base camps over here to comply with new strategies drawn up between President Roosevelt and Winston Churchill to stifle the Nazi ongoing control of European countries. There was an American base set up in Burton at Branston, one of Burton's outskirts, and the Branston pickle factory on the Branston Road was converted into an ordinance depot for supplies, and we got lots of supplies from the Americans during the war.

Between the turn of the New Year and the run up to Easter, we used to visit Grandma and Grandad Skivington a lot, who lived at 62 Broadway Street, just off the top end of Uxbridge Street, about a mile walk from Dale

Street. Also Aunty Tess Skivington, who was an ex-dancer on the stage and was married to my Uncle Tom who was at war in the tank corps (desert rat) and was my Mam's eldest brother. They had two sons: cousin Derek, thirteen and Terry, seven. They lived on Napier Street, also just off the top end of Uxbridge Street, but on the right-hand side. Aunty Flo, Mam's eldest sister, who was also the eldest child of the Skivingtons, lived on Branston Road. She was married then to a chap called Ernie, I think. I remember him well and I liked him, but they split up after the war. I don't know why, but I don't remember anyone speaking badly of him, not even Aunty Flo and she moaned about everything and was always saying how ill she was, what with her bad back, dizzy spells and you name it, she had it (and guess what? Yep. She outlived them all), but she was okay really and I got to know her kinder side later.

Aunty Evelyn, Mam's younger sister, lived with Grandma and Grandad and was married to Bill Kent who was my Dad's younger brother and serving in the Royal Artillery at war. Also living at my Grandparents' was my Uncle Phil, but he was away at war in the army. He was my Mam's middle brother (good footballer) and her youngest brother was my Uncle Charlie. He didn't go to war because he worked in the coalmines like my Grandad used to. I think he got married young and had twins, boy and girl, and lived in Nuneaton, near Burton. I know Mam always felt close to him and protective towards him. He used to come and visit us quite a lot. I liked him and when he sang you could hear Nat King Cole.

Apart from our visits around, we also had a lot of visitors and Alma's friends would always be around who seemed to have more tolerance toward me than my sister did. They liked my drawings and paintings, but I would always hide my embroidery and knitting. Yes, I did that. And I couldn't say it was Mam's because she was such an expert at both; she was so good at that kind of work and she would always have some tapestry on the go. I also enjoyed sitting around the open fire talking, listening to the wireless and music on a winter's night, doing these things. I also realised that I got to stay up a bit later if I was occupied in something useful and, anyway, it was cold upstairs.

So most of the time was spent indoors, except for plenty of visits to and from relations, shopping, wheeling and dealing, and we would all congregate at Grandad and Grandmas' house (Arthur and Beatrice) on Saturday nights and see anyone who might be on leave, talk about the war and read out any letters, if any, from the men, and chat about old times when they were young. I and my cousins loved the old stories of when our parents were kids and, as my cousins grew by numbers over the years, we always loved the same old stories over and over, and they always got better and better. Ha-ha. Then most times Grandad would play a tune for us on his violin and make us all cry as he was so good. I suppose with the war going on it made these family moments priceless even at my age and made me feel nice all over to be part of such a good family.

Then sometimes my cousin, Derek, would play something on his violin that Grandad had given him and was teaching him how to play and read music. He would get a good round of applause; he got to be quite good but then he stopped, probably because he joined the Royal Navy, as nobody likes to hear the same passage played over and over again on any musical instrument, as in when practising, especially in the armed forces in confined areas like a ship (overboard) barrack room (shot going over the top) airplane (skydive without a 'chute).

Derek and I have always had a very special friendship. We are both a bit mad; we love gymnasium, keeping fit, martial arts, working out; name it, and we will have bought the tee-shirt between us. Bless him, he is now at the time of this writing, still running the Burton Judo club with his daughter, my lovely niece, Jane, and teaching on the mat. And so he should. He is only 87 and still has big biceps and a washboard tummy, or six-pack as they say these days.

Grandma and Grandads' house was like the flagship of the family where we would visit all the time, plus it was still home to Aunty Evelyn and Uncle Phil when he was on leave, and any overflow would stay with Aunty Flo who had two spare rooms, or us. Our home was popular because Mam always laid on the main Christmas parties and special events, as she was good at it and loved doing it.

During the week, my Grandad worked at Bass Charrington making the oak staves for the beer barrels. I think he was called a sawyer; he would cut and shape the wooden oak staves and pass them onto the Coopers who would trim and fit them together with metal circular bands to form and make beer barrels. It was very skilled work requiring a five-year apprenticeship. He used to work down the coal mines as a younger man and his back was tattooed in blue flecks where coal flakes had fallen from the ceiling and struck him on his back. I remember Grandma commenting on how they accumulated over time, as she always washed him down in his bath each night when he got home, so tired. He used to walk six miles to the pit and back. On his job at the brewery he only had to travel two miles each way on his push bike. And if he called in the pub on the way home, it would literally be a 'push' bike. But this would not happen often, as they used to get an allowance of two pints of beer per day and Grandad used to like to bring his home (where Grandma would have dinner ready). So he would cycle home with a bottle in each hip pocket. I remember seeing them on occasions: ordinary pint bottles with a cork in the top.

Before we leave Grandma and Grandads' house on Broadway Street, there are another couple of incidents worth a mention that happened during this year of 1942.

Grandad Skivington made himself a lovely wooden wheelbarrow for his nice long back garden. It was a good job, as it would be for a man used to working in wood; not just a square DIY barrow, but with nicely shaped tops and strong wooden cleats to hold it together. Everyone admired it inside the shed, and all the grown-ups were saying things like, "seems a shame to put dirt into it

- would look nice polished and with flowers in it". Everyone seemed in good humour and it wasn't until walking home and we turned the corner at the bottom of Broadway Street, then everyone started laughing out loud. Alma said to me that Grandad could not get his new barrow out through the shed door as it was too big. Then I could see why it was funny, but Grandad had another side to him - he didn't mind the joke being on him, but nobody pushed him too far.

The other story is that Uncle Bill was home on leave and decided to prune Grandad's pear tree for him as it was getting overgrown and not bearing good fruit, and Uncle Bill said, 'That firewood will last you a long time.'

Everyone was happy, until my Dad came home on leave and put the dampers on things by announcing, 'That pear tree will never see another pear.'

He was right. It never got cut down and it never sprouted another twig or even a leaf, but just stood there in silent defiance, like an Indian totem pole, year after year.

Poor Uncle Bill. Every time he saw it must have made him wince. Never mind - he didn't get many things wrong in his life, bless him.

Well, Easter was looming up and we were trying to save our sweet coupons. Most Easter stuff was home-made in those days and I used to love painting pictures onto hard boiled eggs, and helping Mam making pastries and gingerbread men and, by now, we were getting some extra supplies off the Americans, who were setting up a base in Burton. They would come around in their trucks, handing out dried milk, chocolate powder and all kinds of stuff. I was allowed out the front a bit more now, so long as I was supervised, and sometimes the Leedhams would have a visitor who came from a place called Two Gates, near Tamworth. She brought two little girls with her and we used to play, mostly in the big yard and inside the cattle open trailer that was usually full of hay. They used to come over a lot and always called for me and I always enjoyed seeing them.

I also used to get invited around to play with a little girl who lived two doors along. We were both on our own doorsteps and we used to wave at each other. Then one day she asked her mum if I could go round to play with her and her mum checked with my Mam who was fine with that, so I took some small items to play with and we played together in her back yard. This happened several times until I started school, and we became good little friends. Their name was Miller. I can't remember the little girl's name, but her father was a fireman, so she had both of her parents at home. I remember she was very pretty, looked and sang like Shirley Temple and she was always top of the bill on all the street parties during the war. They used to set her up with a big microphone and she was not phased or shy - very professional. Everyone made a big fuss of her and her mum and dad spoiled her. She was always turned out like a film star, but she wasn't like that and the short friendship I had with her was nice. Her parents wanted the best for their only child and I am surprised they even allowed a little scruff like me to play with her. Mind you, I was not turned out too badly myself then, and was well-spoken except for a slight lisp. But very soon a couple of years on the streets would soon sort that.

It was about this time that I discovered I could get a lot of attention by throwing myself over and off the furniture. I seemed to be very strong and agile and I loved going to the pictures, where I saw Charlie Chaplin. I was so impressed by his antics and gymnastics that I began to copy him and it seemed to come natural to me, plus no speaking was required; being a shy-ish boy it became a good outlet for me. And the first time I tested it out on my mum was one day she came in with some washing to hang on the clothes rack that hung from the living room ceiling above the fire, and would be lowered up and down by a sash cord rope on a pulley, and she was hanging some shirts and light stuff over the rails. I stood on top of the arm of the settee facing inwards stood upright and shouted 'Mam!'

As she turned with her arm full of washing, I was falling backwards to the floor. She threw the washing in a chair and came rushing over to find me giggling on the floor. She just came down with me and made me laugh more by tickling me. I was always very ticklish and still am. So was Mam, especially around the neck and she would beg me to stop, and I remember many, many years later, when she was on heart tablets, I held my hands forward, reaching toward her neck and she started chuckling and said, 'Don't you dare - you will kill me.'

Anyway we got up and she said, 'Show me how you did that.'

So I did; then I showed her some others that I had been practising, like putting my weight on one leg and kicking it away with the free leg to fall sideways, backwards and forwards. She loved it and told me to be very careful. That's what I loved about my folks, although we never wanted, we were not wrapped up in cotton wool. So I continued practising my tumbling until it became a lifestyle and a big part of my life and career.

I used to love going to the pictures. I liked anything, especially if it was in colour: cowboys, adventure films, like *Robin Hood*, and pirate films with exotic fruit in bowls, like I had never seen in real life, (like the hero would bite into a peach and the whole audience would go whoare as the juice trickled down his chin) and the old black and white comedy films as a second 2ⁿᵈ feature and always a cartoon, plus the Walt Disney main features - superb. *Dumbo* was my first 1ˢᵗ great. Each one was a masterpiece, and a bag of chips on the way home with salt and vinegar on and to be eaten in the British traditional manner out of the newspaper with fingers whilst walking along the street, and if you saw someone you knew really, really, really, knew you could offer them a chip. I heard people talking about the war and our lads being away miles from home and longing for peace. But apart from the talk, the wireless, the *Movietone News* at the pictures and, of course, the air raids, most of us kids did not do too badly considering and, at my age, I did not know any different. So when I look back, I do so admire the grown-ups of then for their sheer balls and determination to pull together to get through and, although the Americans were now in with us, the war was not going well for us at this time.

Japs were taking over the Philippines.

Combined force ABDA was set up to deal with the problems in the West Pacific.

Singapore surrendered and 80,000 Commonwealth troops were taken prisoner.

Japanese first air attack on Australian mainland at Darwin, 135 aircraft killing 240 people. Followed by almost 100 raids during 1942-43.

A failed attempt to stop the Japanese attacking Java i.e. Battle of Java Sea.

General MacArthur was ordered to leave the Philippines for Darwin, Australia by the US President.

Allied forces surrendered at Bataan and the Philippines fell to Japan.

78,000 Filipino and American prisoners of war started the sixty-five-mile Bataan Death March.

Britain was still getting hammered from the air to try and halt our hardworking factories and our mass production lines. I think they had given up wasting ammo trying to break our spirit and morale, realising it just made us worse. We would stick our finger in the air shout, "bugger off"; write some more daft songs about it; sing them all the time; make up some good jokes about it.

That's another thing I love about the Brits: they know how to laugh at themselves and you can't explain British humour to an outsider. I mean it isn't rocket science is it, and some of the songs and words had to be written whilst drunk; they were so awful they were great - no wonder they live on? I mean *Chickery Chick*; *Run Rabbit*; *The Good Ship Lollipop*; *The Laughing Policeman*.

Well, my birthday was good I got cards, presents, cake, etc. One present I remember was Teddy who always went to bed with me along with my rag doll Pixie that I already had. I still had Teddy into my teens; then he was passed onto Alastair, my first nephew, and Pixie ended up in the dog basket with our new dog, Betty. She was a black Manchester terrier cross, very fit and smart and, of course, I loved her. We also had a new cat called Bubbles who was very smart and got treated like a person; the only difference was he never did anything wrong, ha - probably because he didn't. He was a great cat, pure white short hair except for two black spots, one each side of his body, a heart shaped black patch on his forehead finishing to a point just above his eyes and a black tip to his tail and all of his markings were so even you'd think they'd been painted on.

Now with Easter behind us, Alma, who had sailed through her secondary selection exams, had started at the Burton Technical High School, and I was ready for the infants' school, sort of.

I vaguely remember my first day at school. Alma dropped me off at Uxbridge St. School Infants entrance on the left side facing of the main school with the duty teacher who was standing at the front wall entrance holding a bell. She gave me a kiss and strode off in the ongoing direction towards her tech. school. I was led into the infants' playground and encouraged to play with the other children until the bell rang. They all looked a bit unsure, like me. And I know I wasn't really worried about much; it was nice to see so many other children and a few were playing in small groups and seemed to already know each other.

Then the bell rang and everyone stopped and looked at the bell ringer, as if we already knew that was the thing to do. It was the young lady who was standing at the front entrance when we all arrived. Apparently she was the orderly teacher of the day. Then she was joined by two other teachers and we were sorted into three lines and asked to pretend that we were soldiers whilst the teachers lined us up and swapped us around to end up with three evenly chosen ranks of short, medium and tall boys and girls. Then we were told to remember which row we were in and who was in front of you so that when the bell sounds off in the morning that is where you go, and also if you are asked to form up at any other time in the playground on the playing field or in the big hall. I think we were just called rows one, two, three from left to right.

We were then told to always be quiet and put up your hand if you wanted to speak or needed the toilet, etc. Then we had a guided tour. We had our own small playground with some play items in it; toilets at the end of the playground with tiny toilet pans. There was a large tin roof lean-to running from the toilets to the first classroom and ran along the wall that separated the infants from the main school. And this area was used for bikes and other storage and also housed a lock-up for sports stuff. At the end side was a big green gate that led into the school playing field and air raid shelters.

Next we were led into a large classroom where we were joined by the headmistress. She was a real old lady of around 45-ish, who greeted us new intakes, told us what a great school it was and what to do for a fire alert and air raids of which we would have some drill and practice over the next few days. And we did (good fun). She also introduced us to a couple of evacuees who had joined us at school and asked us all to welcome them and be nice to them. I thought "right mate, join the queue".

That's about all I remember of my first day at school. I think Mam collected me and all was well and I think that I must have decided not to leave school just yet.

7

My second day at school is much more memorable as when Alma dropped me off at the front gate she spotted a couple of her own school chums walking to school, so they all shouted to each other and she ran across the road to join up with them. In doing so she forgot to kiss me, so my bottom lip started to go out as it so often did far too easily and, by the time I was in the playground, I was bawling my eyes out. I was still blubbing away when we went into the classroom. The other kids were looking at me with concern and wondering where I was injured. When the teacher asked what was wrong and I told her that my big sister did not kiss me goodbye at the school gate, the other kids fell about laughing and I was trying to laugh with them because, although I was upset, I also knew if it was one of them I would laugh too.

Anyway, the teacher gave me a hug and made me feel okay and told the other kids to look through the new books on their desks.

Then she said to me, 'Look, I have a newish jumper here - was left by someone from last term and they never came back for it.' So she tried it on me and my hands disappeared and it nearly came down to my knees. It would have fitted Arnold Schwarzenegger.

She said, 'Oh, it's far too big, isn't it?' and I said, 'I will grow into it,' thinking it would be okay for Alma or Mam. But it wasn't to be.

Although that incident was embarrassing, it did seem to set me off on a good footing with my first ever teacher. She knew I liked her and I was never shy to ask her advice or questions and sometimes she would ruffle my hair which was always sticking up as she walked by. She tried to encourage me to use my right hand; so did some of the other teachers. But I was always a lefty - left handed and left footed. I tried hard to use my right hand to be like my Uncle Bill, who could use both equally well but favoured his left. But I was never forced like he was. I took a bit of stick along the way from the other kids, like "Did you get your kiss today?" or "Kiss me quick", but it didn't really bother me and I have never minded taking and giving a bit of goading now and again. It wasn't too long before they found out that there was another side to this little softy. I say little, because although I was stocky I was very short.

The second day at school was okay. I think we did another air raid and fire practice. We did these quite frequently because at this time during the war we never knew what to expect. After that day I don't think Alma and I ever kissed again as children. I didn't look for one and it never came. From then on, it wasn't long before I was going to school on my own, which was great as I didn't know how to walk anywhere. We would pick up with each other along the way and amble along back home in the afternoons. Our parents weren't too worried as there were lots of us and not much traffic. Motor driving was different then. No one did speed in the towns unless police or a fire engine and they made so much noise with bells and sirens, you would know. Plus most things on the road would be either a delivery vehicle with a load of something, or the odd car if someone was lucky enough to have one (and the petrol to put in it which was on tight rationing). It would probably be an old banger that the Army didn't want, in dire need of a couple of unavailable parts and bald tyres with the inner tube showing. Quite legal then, meaning it would have to be driven with care. And we would be running down Uxbridge Street like a bunch of Gremlins.

Speaking of Gremlins, I used to love playing with all the other kids and playtime was horrendous - the noise we used to make, and some kids went home for dinner (at lunchtime) but I didn't; I had dinner at school. I loved my school dinners and always a pudding, having always been a pig up until this day, I used to eat mine as fast as possible as there was nearly always second helpings. I would get some more (please sir). Most of the kids had no table manners at all so that gave me an excuse to behave like them, and eat the way I like and, who knows, perhaps some of them were doing the same. Ha-ha. I saw a lad licking his plate clean one day and I just managed to resist the temptation to copy him. My snobby sister would have been proud of me.

It was good for Mam now that I was at school, as she had taken a job, working at a small factory called The Black Cat, a ten-minute walk from home, making ammunition. She was learning to be a capstan turner, so she would only have to make tea during the week.

Once I was settled in at school, I was allowed to play in the street until Alma came home from school, but I had to stay in Dale Street. My Aunty May used to be at our house until Alma got home and I had to report to her when I got home from school. She was not my real aunty but a good friend of my Mam and became Alma's mother-in-law.

About halfway through my first term, I acquired my first girlfriend. I can't remember how it all came about - I don't think she was even in my class. She was in the same year as me but we were split into two groups and had different classrooms most of the time, because when I came out of school she was always at the school gate before me waiting for me to join her. We used to hold hands and walk down Uxbridge Street together. I think we used to meet up in the playground and I remember that she was always dressed smartly and clean and good at speaking. I remember one afternoon in the summer of 1942, walking hand in hand with my girlfriend when she spotted a sweet on the railway crossing that used to run across Uxbridge St, so she bent down, picked it up released my hand and began to unwrap it, to which I said, 'Don't eat that, it's dirty.' So she popped it in her mouth and said, 'It's nice and it was wrapped up.' I find it very strange that the sweet incident remains so prominent in my memory. We were only tots but I know in our way that we loved each other. I don't think we ever kissed, even when I dropped her outside her home just before Dale Street.

A few days later she gave me some bad news and told me that she was having to leave Burton with her mum to live in another town. I don't know why, and I don't think she knew why, as we were only tots. We didn't know how to swap numbers and we couldn't even write yet, so I dropped her home and never saw her again; she was so pretty. Bloody War.

8

We are now well into 1942. I am settled in at school and I like it very much, especially drawing, painting, PT (PE) games, story times, playtimes and dinner times, but I don't much like putting letters and names to fruit and animals and trying to write and read things. That is when I go into my shell because I realise that I am behind most of the other children on this part of my education and it worries me a little bit because I really want to learn and read lots of books like my big sister; she always has her head in a book.

Meanwhile street life was good and I was beginning to meet up with all kinds of scruffs and share our toys and bits of food or sweets. Sometimes some Americans would be around from their base at Branston and we would shout, 'Got any gum chum?', and they would always throw us some packs of chewing gum. Their gum was in long strips. Ours was gum inside a white mint coated tablet. We used to get loads of goodies and supplies from the Americans and they were always nice and friendly, and when they came to town they were issued with all sorts of stuff to hand out to the locals. Sometimes they would pull up in a jeep or a truck to go around the streets handing out free supplies, including silk stockings mostly carried inside a tunic pocket. I wasn't sure why.

We loved the Yanks, and they looked like film stars in their really smart uniforms. No wonder our lads weren't very happy about them being over here whilst they were away and our blokes who were not in the war who thought they had the pick of the bunch during the war made up the famous slogan, those Yanks "Overpaid Oversexed and Over here". But it would have been a different war without them and, at that time, they were helping to support and guard our island. They were doing regular bombing raids on German targets and rehearsing for the largest amphibian battle landing ever. I know we kids loved to see them. Even if they did bomb our town a couple of times whilst practising their bombing skills and accidentally used live ammo called friendly fire.

When I got home from school I would go through the small wicket door of the big wooden front gates, go and give Beauty a hug, who would be wagging his or her tail I don't think I ever knew what sex he was. I loved him anyway. Then I would report in the house to Aunty May or Alma, have a drink of water, scrounge something to eat like an apple, and shoot out to play.

On the way I would say hello to Betty the dog, Bubbles the cat, and sometimes the chickens that we now had at the end of the garden, following the repairs to the original chicken run and front wire and door, that Dad carried out on his last leave. This was butted up to Dad's shed with a chicken wire and frame door in a frame and wire panel fixed between the shed front and the boundary wall, up to the end wall with a wooden coop at the back end of the shed. The whole area was about three yards by five yards.

Sometimes I would help Alma feed the chickens with some stuff out of a large bag. It was called meal and you would mix it with hot water until it looked like brown porridge. We would also save all our veg peelings, stale bread and anything that they would eat and chuck it all in together. They loved it.

Also, we usually had a couple of rabbits in two hutches which sat on top of a large stone slab that was fitted into the corner of the outside walls of the WC and the boundary wall with a single brick wall support under each end, thus forming an alcove underneath, where we would keep straw, hay, sawdust, etc. which was never a problem for us having cattle merchants for neighbours.

And the high boundary wall ran along the back from the toilet end wall to the end of the chicken run where it cornered across to meet up with our fence boundary line. And behind our far end boundary line was still Leedham's property, and behind Dad's shed, Jack Leedham had built a brick boiler where he would boil up stuff from the farms to add to his pig swill and he was always filling it with potatoes and I often would see him and his men selecting a nice roast potato and they would walk around the yard eating them.

So when I was a bit older, it did not take me too long to pick up on the idea of having a couple of mates around where we would lie on the top of Dad's shed roof: a flat sloping felt roof, where we could lie down and see over the top of the boundary wall into the backs of all the other houses and, from the roof, we could reach over to grab the roast potatoes. And on a dark night when I was allowed out till later, especially when my Mam was on night shifts, we would lie on the shed roof enjoying our roast spuds takeaway and giggling as we puffed on a shared roll-up fag, knowing that the smoke from a cig would get blamed on the boiler that was still warm.

I think that we acquired the chickens at Easter time. I remember they arrived in a cardboard box and were all little fluffy chicks and Alma and I looked after them mostly. Alma and I would keep them with fresh water. For a while they were kept in the fire hearth in a cardboard box and we would keep changing their hay and straw. I remember that there were a lot of them. I can't remember if we lost any but they were in the pen now. We had a rooster called Tweedle-Dum, and a laying hen called Tweedle-Dee; they were Rhode Island Reds. I don't know if they were in the same batch or came separate. I just remember that those two were with us to the last kill, and Tweedle-Dum grew up to outwit me many times.

Anyway, I was getting more worldly now, meeting other new kids on the block, so to speak, and we all had a little play on the street after school before getting called in for tea; then most of us younger ones would have to stay in our homes to get cleaned up and ready for school next day. I would normally have to go to bed between 7:30 and 8pm, depending how long I could make my light supper last and how distracted the powers-that-be were. Sometimes I would get Mam into conversation or be allowed to finish some section of embroidery or darning I was on. But when Mam started night shifts at the ammo factory there was no chance with Alma; she didn't like talking to me anyway, only to tell me off for something, except for the odd occasion when she would have her head buried in a book, and I would have to be so quiet that it really wasn't worth it, and it didn't really matter to me because I always fell asleep straightaway and, short of an air raid, wouldn't wake up until called next morning, (Christmas and birthdays were exceptions).

I was always good at getting up in the morning; one call and I am up; didn't always want to get up, but still did it. We were disciplined in those days and it has stayed with me all my life: school, apprenticeship, Army, Civvy Street, etc. It's more a case of self-discipline than doing what you're told. You know you have something to do, so get up and let's do it. Most of the kids that lived around me went to Christ Church School, and that was just around the corner of Dale Street and closer for me. I am not sure why I didn't go there but I am glad I went to Uxbridge Street School, because it was a good school, and bigger with more facilities. The only problem with my slow progress was me, not the school, plus Alma went there and most of our relations lived around that area, and my older cousins may have gone there. If I was early I would sometimes call for one of my new friends who lived en route just around the corner which was out of my house, go left, walk forty yards to the end of the street, turn left at the corner shop (Cracker Law, the barber, learned how to cut hair in the Army - need I say more).

He only used hand clippers. He only did one cut – I can't say style and we were all told that he had a pudding basin in his shop that he would put on your head and cut off what hair he could see. I don't know, I never went there, and I don't know anyone else who did except my Uncle Tom who didn't mind looking as if he was in the Foreign Legion, and was a mate of his.

But Cracker Law did sell other things, as most shops did during the war, and I believe he did a good trade in French Letters and carried a large stock, but of course I did not know any of this yet. Anyway, left at the corner shop onto Uxbridge Street; then left and through the first entry and the first house on the left was the back of my friend's house. His mam would be helping him with his shoes and socks and combing his hair with water.

Once his mam said to me, 'Do you dress yourself Gordon?'

I said, 'Yes'

'And can you tie your own shoe laces?'

I said, 'Yes,' and she said that I was very good.

Then I remembered my new friend, Michael, added, 'Yes, but he can't tell the time like me.' and she said, 'Is that true?' to which I said again, 'Yes'. I think she was happy with that.

We became good pals and I got on with his parents very well and I was to go around to his house to play quite a lot. His dad was a train driver. And I would often see him in his uniform and when he came home. He would smell of smoke and oil, but it was a good smell. To be an engine driver was like being a spaceman today, plus I only found out recently that one of my great grandfathers was a train driver.

Michael and I were always mates, but we seemed to part company in junior school due to the grading system; he went up as I went down, and I think he ended up at grammar school, plus he was more spoiled than me and I don't think his folks would have liked him mixing with the wonderful little sods that I did.

So the year of '42 was passing along okay for me. Grandad had made a new front to his shed, with a wider door on it. Uncle Phil had been captured by the Germans and had escaped from a works party by jumping from a cliff into a river. He was fired on, but not hit. I remember him laughing when he told us the story at Grandad's, and saying what lousy shots them Jerrys were, but many years later I was to find out that firing downwards with a rifle is not easy, and if they were in charge of a prisoners' works party they would only be ordinary squaddies and not trained to kill.

Anyway, he did very well to get himself back to his lines and the jump could have killed him, but he was a fit lad and a good footballer, and came from a mad family and got himself a leave; then they sent him back to more action for being so brave, but not to worry. My Dad, Uncles, Bill, Tom, Phil and Arthur all saw action in WW2 and all came back.

Whilst at school, I was learning nursery rhymes and popular folk songs. I hated singing as I only had a small range and open key was too high a pitch for me, plus I was very shy, so always felt it embarrassing. But all in all, school was great fun and I wasn't too worried about stuff I couldn't do very well.

Meanwhile the war raged on.

January: Japanese troops enter Manila, capital of the Philippines. Japanese invade Burma. Africa Corps Germany (Rommel) march from El-Agheila to El-Alamain.

February: Singapore surrenders to the Japanese. MacArthur ordered to leave Bataan by the US President.

March: British citizens and troops are evacuated from Rangoon, Burma. First Jews arrive at Auschwitz.

April: All Jews in Europe ordered to wear the "Star of David"

May: End of the American armed resistance on the Philippines. Large American Expeditionary Force reaches Northern Ireland. Mexico declares war on Germany, Italy, and Japan.

June: 1047 bombers raid on Cologne, Germany by the RAF.

9

So we pick up on my story from the middle of 1942.

It was a great summer and during the school holidays Mam, Alma and I used to go on lots of picnics. We would often meet up with friends and relations especially on Sundays.

We would go mostly to the Ox Hay which was a large recreation field that had a long footbridge that went all the way over the edge of the field until it joined up with a large, wider iron suspension bridge that reached over the river Trent.

This led into an area called Stapenhill and at the end of the bridge there was a shop that sold ice cream and a boat hire mooring. Sometimes, when the men were home, we would hire a row boat and take our picnic along the river and moor up along the bank any place you liked.

I would often take a fishing net and a jam jar to catch some tiddlers, if there was room, because with my Mam a picnic meant an outdoor banquet. She would even spread a tablecloth out over the grass. So everyone had to carry something on the way there.

If we didn't hire a boat, which was most times, we would sit near the river, sometimes under the trees, if it was hot. It was also handy for a pee, in particular when my cousins came along and the lemonade was flowing.

Sometimes, when there was a good crowd of us, the men would have a bottle of beer and a smoke and everyone would be laughing and joking and you could see other people over and around the field having picnics, playing football, cricket, running around playing - you would never think that there was a bitter war for our survival going on.

At the end of the Ox Hay field was a large metal gate that led into an area called the Cherry Orchard. In this area were swings, a roundabout, a slide and a water pump with a heavy half-pint brass goblet that hung on a chain. When you held the goblet under the spout and pumped the metal arm up and down it would fill up with the most beautiful cold spring water I have ever tasted in my life. I know the brass goblet was used by all and sundry and I am usually very fussy about such things but, in this case, it didn't seem to matter, though I would always wipe the area from which I was about to drink. It was as if you had to use that special cup with the magic water and was to save my life many times in the future when I was older; running through the woods that ran along the edge of the Ox Hay, to escape the wild animals in there, or the sheriff of Nottingham, or the Ox Hay desert and even a game of football. And, for as long as I can remember, that pump and brass mug was always there without damage.

The Ox Hay was a good fun place, not just for kids to play and have adventures, but during the war they would lay on all kinds of things like small shows, side stalls, sports events and football. I suppose it was treated like a massive park and, although there was a keeper, restrictions were quite loose and, when I got a bit older, we used to tie ropes on the trees, build camps, make dens in the woods and have small camp fires. We did pretty much what we liked in the woods, especially during the war years, and there were no health and safety rules then. I loved the danger in the woods: running, jumping, climbing trees and you soon learned how to jump from one branch to another without missing. I think it's a good way to grow up; you get to know your own measure and limitations and when not to push your luck. Like when to be brave but not stupid.

The long footbridge mentioned several pages ago is called the Stapenhill footbridge. On the other side of the iron suspension bridge there was a road and a couple of walkways. We would often take the left turn at the end of the bridge and go along what was called the New Walk where there were beautiful trees and plants and flowers and fish ponds, etc. All of which I did not appreciate at all, as I was usually the only child in the group, all dressed up in my Sunday best and not allowed to play or get dirty.

Picnics and walking were very popular in those days. But when you think about it, these things were healthy, great for conversation, meeting up with others, courting couples, looking for girls who were looking for boys, showing off how smart you could be on a Sunday, and enjoying the river life. I was a bit young then to appreciate most of that and it did me no harm. I am not surprised that all these lovely things were so popular. It was all relatively free, and no one had any real money in those days. But it did not stop me having a sense of relief when I later started Sunday school, so was excused the Sunday walks. Not that Sunday school was a walk in the park either, as I will explain later in my story.

Sometimes on these walks, I would collect pieces of wood to make miniature items with when I got home; like bows and arrows, dolls' house furniture, etc. Alma used to collect flowers and leaves and press them in books. Times were good for me - then suddenly I became quite ill. I don't remember exactly when, but I contracted something called Bright's disease. Bright's Disease, as it was referred to years ago, is problems with the kidneys, now called Glomerulonephritis. I think Bright is the name of the man who pioneered many of the discoveries of the kidney functions and treatments to prevent kidney failure, and their functions are vital to the human body.

I can remember being very poorly and I was set up in Mam's bedroom with a fire on. I felt very weak and tired, but I don't remember any pain. I do remember seeing a couple of large coloured circles even when my eyes were closed, and when I told this to my Mam, she said that would be the angels watching over you (she was quite religious); then when I said 'yes' and I was up there with them last night looking down on myself, she looked quite startled as she knew I never lied. This happened to me a couple of times during this period, and Mam was always telling people about my 'out of body experience'.

This and similar experiences have happened to me about six or seven times during my life and always when very tired, half asleep or on medication, so I am open minded about why. It can be very vivid, but then so can hallucinations.

The doctor came to see me every day. I remember him well. His name was Dr Gillis. He was of medium height, always wore a suit and looked very important with his small 'tache. He was pleasant and was our family doctor for years and Mam got on with him well. I suppose we had to pay the doctor in those days, as there was no NHS then. People would look upon a doctor's visit as a need to have a spring clean.

After a while, I was moved back into the large front bedroom, still with a fire, though, so I must have been on the mend then. I was probably put in Mam's room because it was cosier and quiet at the back, except for Tweedle-Dum in the mornings. So I was on the mend, but I had been very poorly. I don't know exactly what was wrong but there were some complications and Mam told me in later years that I'd had a close call. She was told that I might not be able to keep up with the other kids and that I could be a sickly child and to keep an eye on me to always wear a vest and keep warm.

She told me all these things a few years later when I received a medal for being the junior champion gymnast at the Burton

YMCA. One problem I did have after my illness was that my left eye would go into the inner corner when I tried to focus on anything, so had to have eye tests and was fitted with a pair of specs. The left lens was opaque at first in the hope that the left eye would relax and return to normal but this did not happen and without my glasses on I could only see double vision until I pulled my eye into the corner in order to focus, which was a strain on the eye. So I was fitted with a proper clear lens which kept my eyes straight and in focus, and I had to wear glasses until I was twenty years old.

How I hated them for so many reasons. But why was I moaning? I was lucky to be around. I was making a fast recovery. Plenty of picture shows, enjoying the wireless more, making things at home, and Christmas was around the corner.

I think I had to take it easy for a while after my illness. I don't remember much of it, but I spent a lot of time in the house listening to the wireless and making things, as I loved using my hands. I loved all music, even classical and opera, and was always asking if I could play the piano, but was not allowed. It was Alma's, and she was having lessons and had to practice her exercises for a half hour every day. I was not allowed to watch her because I put her off. I didn't think she was much cop, and she knew it.

Mam wasn't too bad on it, until I realised one day that she played the same bass left hand for everything (ha!) and every tune was in the same tempo, but she swung it well. She was self-taught and it always went down well at party times when there was no real piano player around (bless), and she was under no illusions, having come from a musical family.

Her singing was exceptional and she could easily have become a professional singer. I'm sure my early memories are so happy because Mam was always singing in the background whilst she did her housework, and she was gifted with perfect pitch.

Alma, on the other hand, did not seem to have much real interest in music and she did not pursue beyond her exercises and a couple of small pieces of light music; so they may as well have let me loose on the piano after all. It looked like Alma took after my Dad's side of the family for her mild interest in music. Even Dad's whistling only had two notes, and they were always in the wrong places, but I must say that was an achievement, as in those days he would have probably had a woodbine hanging from his mouth at the same time, whilst gardening or chiselling away at a piece of wood.

He was like a beaver always doing something or making something and that was when he was happy. I loved it when he was happy; he was such a good man, and a real man.

So it is now closing to Christmas 1942. And the War continues.

April – Tobruk captured by Rommel's Panzer Army. He was promoted by Hitler to Field Marshall. 35,000 Allied troops surrendered, and General Auchinleck takes over direct command of the British Eighth Army in North Africa.

27th June. – Convoy PQ17 sails from Iceland for Archangel, it includes 33 merchant ships.

28th June – 7,000 prisoners from the Eighth Army are captured by Rommel.

4th July – Convoy PQ17 is attacked by German torpedo bombers and dive-bombers. Two merchant ships sunk and two more damaged. The Admiralty gave the order to scatter the convoy.

5th July – Germany launches an all-out assault on Convoy PQ17.

10th July – Only two out of the 33 ships reach Archangel. More will arrive in the following days. (23 of these ships are still missing to this day along with 430 tanks, 210 planes, 3,500 vehicles and nearly 100,000 tons of cargo).

7th Aug – Americans land at Guadacanal.

13th Aug – Monty gives private speech to English Army Officers before El Alamein. Which included his famous speech "Here we will stand and fight".

17th Aug – The attack on Dieppe begins a day late due to bad weather at British ports.

19th Aug – The Dieppe Raid sees more than 6,000 mainly Canadian troops suffer a casualty rate of 70% before the decision was made to call a retreat, some six hours later.

23rd Aug – The German Army reaches the banks of the river Volga in Stalingrad.

25th Aug – Heavy Russian fighting halts the German advance in Stalingrad.

13th Sept – The Japanese launch a major offensive against the Americans at Guadalcanal but sustain heavy casualties.

23rd Oct – British forces attack the German army at El Alamein in North Africa.

4th Nov – The German army in North Africa is in full retreat, after suffering a comprehensive defeat at El Alamein, Egypt, at the hands of the British Eighth Army under General Bernard Montgomery.

8th Nov – The start of Operation Torch – the Allied invasion of North Africa. Allied troops land near Casablanca, Oran and Algiers. With a large Allied army in the west of North Africa and with Monty advancing from the east, Rommel is caught between two major forces.

24th Nov – After weeks of heavy fighting, the Russians launch an attack that encircles the Germans at Stalingrad.

12th Dec – The Germans launch Operation Winter Storm to relieve their army in Stalingrad. It fails after eleven days, leaving the V1 Army trapped.

31st Dec – The Japanese plan to withdraw their troops from Guadalcanal after suffering heavy losses in a number of battles.

10

So back home Christmas went well, as it always does. Alma and I each had our pillowcase full of presents plus always a special one. I think mine was roller skates this year as I was desperate to have a pair just like the bigger boys. I was getting tough again and had seen a couple of Charlie Chaplin films whom I loved to watch and copy his antics and tumbling.

Mam had one of her usual Christmas parties with lots of food and trimmings for family and friends. I don't know how she did it during the war, but she did, and always without any stress or panic. I think because she enjoyed it so. In fact, she played a big part in holding us all together during and after the war, including Grandma and Grandad and was known throughout as our Ep, Aunty Ep, or Epee.

The only other thing I remember about this Christmas was I did something that annoyed Aunty Flo - which was not difficult. My cousins and I were all scared of her; she was like a headmistress and always looked stern and was the eldest of all my Aunts and Uncles. Anyway, she told me off for something, waving her finger at me and I started to cry.

'Stop that crying. I didn't hit you.'

So I stopped crying and couldn't get my breath. I went red in the face, then white and started stamping my feet as my Mam appeared from the other room.

'Stop him doing that, Ethel; that is sheer temper,' said Aunty Flo.

Mam rushed over to me, went down on her knees as I was about to collapse, held me whilst patting me on the back and jumping me up and down; then I suddenly caught a breath and started breathing and sobbing. Aunty Edie (Evelyne) was standing by with a glass of water.

Mam said to me, 'Are you okay now?'

I said "yes"; we had been there before and she knew exactly what to do.

Then she stood up and turned to face Aunty Flo, who blustered, 'I didn't hit him.'

Mam said, 'I know - you just hurt his feelings, and he doesn't have a temper.' Then she walked away.

According to Alma, as I was already in the other room with Aunty Evelyne drinking my water, and feeling stupid again for always crying so easily, I didn't know this outcome. I did feel sorry for Aunty Flo, because although she was a bit of a dragon, she was okay really and the older I got the better we got on.

We are now into 1943, and I am back at school for a new term after the Christmas holidays. I think I went up into the junior school at this time. This was separated from the infants' by a big brick wall and entered through the main front gates that led into what seemed a large playground, full of mad kids all bigger than me.

When the bell went, we were all led into the main hall for what was called assembly, where we would sing a hymn and say the Lord's prayer. Then we were all told to sit, and we would sit cross-legged on the wooden floor, whilst the head teacher or deputy would tell us of any relevant issues. Then we were handed over to our new form teacher for the whole next term by the headmistress. Because we were the new intake we were sat at the front and known as first form juniors. So we were told to stand up and were led out first, and this would continue, one form at a time until the fifth form 10-year-olds at the end would be led out.

We were led into our new classroom, which to me looked very daunting and formal. The desks were made of solid oak and wrought iron framing constructed as a pair of desks. Each desk had a hinged lid to access a box storage compartment for books (catapult, fag cards, new milk tops, marbles, and a broken watch). The seat was slatted oak strips, like on a park bench seat, with no back so that you could be told to sit up all the time. The desk top had a small flat area after the lid hinge for laying ruler, etc, a groove for pen and pencil, a hole called an inkwell and with an end stop to stop things falling off. These desks were very heavy and were all lined up in a straight and orderly fashion. At the front of the classroom was a 'what we then called' a blackboard and easel.

The ceiling was very high. The walls were painted brickwork, as were most of the internal walls of the school. The windows were long and narrow with a point at the top and too high up to see out of; they had to be opened and closed with a long pole with a metal or brass hook on the top end.

I was told to sit at the front because I was short and I felt like a rabbit caught in the headlights, but I got used to it and settled in well, though I was always worried about my learning skills and was very shy in class, but hid that side of myself, I think. As usual though, I loved playtime and school dinners.

It was a mixed school and some of the fifth formers remembered my sister, and one morning we walked past my school together and, as she left me at the school gate to walk on to her tech school, a couple of the older lads said, 'Hello, Marilyn.' which was her first Christian name.

And she said, 'Hello boys - you look after my little brother.' and walked on, as they shouted, 'We will.'

Then they said to me, 'Your sister was head prefect and cock of the school when she was here.'

I thought, I'm not surprised; she may look like a girl, but I knew what it was like to get on the wrong side of her.

I liked school and mixing with all of the other children. I so wanted to read and write like my big sister so that I could read a whole book like she could, but it was not happening. The more I told myself to concentrate, the more my mind would wander. I used to daydream a lot and sometimes the teacher would point at me to answer a question and I would dissolve, as I would be wondering why his tie did not go with his jacket or why did she keep pushing up her sleeves. So I had not a clue what they were talking about and was always behind most of the other kids with my learning. I was also afraid to hold up my hand if I did not understand or hear something in case the other kids laughed at me or realized how far behind them I was - especially in a mixed class.

I didn't mind the boys; I could beat them up, but the girls laughing at me would have embarrassed me too much, so I would blag it as much as possible. Sitting at the front of the classroom and being fairly well spoken and polite would not have helped, so giving the impression that I was bright when I wasn't. In fact I became quite skilled at blagging it and I used this skill throughout my schooldays to get out of lessons that I did not want to do or was useless at, only to lose out in the end by outsmarting myself.

School was mostly great fun. Playtime was usually wild and noisy, good cooked dinners always with a nice proper pudding followed by more playtime. Some children went home for dinner and some would call in their homes after school dinner if they lived close, but I always stayed at school. Once, after school dinner, I was chatting with one of the girls in my class and she said that she wanted to pop home for something - would I like to go with her, so I said yes. She lived very close to the school and was a nice girl, liked by everyone. So, we got to her home and she pulled up the back door key from an outside pot as her mam was at work like most of our parents during the war. The key was just like ours: massive just like a jailor's key, you didn't lose your keys in those days. So she showed me in. It was nice and clean, not unlike my home. Then we went into the back garden, when she suddenly said she needed a number two and would not be long, so I stood out in the back yard near the outside toilet.

Then she said, 'Gordon, will you bring me some newspaper from inside the kitchen - there is none in here.' and I said, 'I daren't in case your mam comes and catches me.'

She said, 'It's okay, she won't mind.' but I bottled out and, in the end, the girl shuffled along her back yard with her knickers around her ankles and back to the WC. She was fine with it and we became good classmates and I went to her house a couple more times afterwards.

I saw her years later at the students' union and we gave each other a wry smile from a distance. She had grown into a pretty young teenager, as I always knew she would. The afternoons in those days were usually good. We would have music, art, reading, story time (class favourite) drama etc. then home time.

I would usually run all the way home, report in to Mam, Alma, or Aunty May, say hello to Beauty, change into my play clothes (not much different from my school clothes as we did not wear uniforms) and no ordinary kids were well dressed during the war. And play clothes would be things that you were growing out of and not good enough to hand on.

Sometimes, if the yard was empty, and Beauty was on his own, I would go and give him a hug and sometimes I would shake the chicken wire to show my appreciation to Tweedle-Dum for his early morning calls. He used to go mad and fly at the wire and I would run away laughing my head off.

Tweedle-Dum was so cocky he would tell the other chickens off, eat their food, squawk at anyone who approached his pen, unless you were carrying a bowl. So he needed me to keep him in check. I loved him really and had seen him grow from a fluffy little yellow thing into this aggressive arrogant cocksure monster he had become. The relationship between Dum and me was a bit like Alma and me. There must be a moral there, maybe (reap what you sow) hem, - get out and play – right.

Out in the street, I was allowed to play between Cracker Laws shop which is about fifty yards to the right coming out of our big gates and on the corner of Dale Street and Uxbridge Street and to the left of our gates as far as Fraser's corner shop, which would be also about fifty yards, and had to be in before dark for tea at around 5pm. But I would normally get called in for tea for which I was always starving hungry. I was usually allowed something out with me after school like a piece of fruit or bread and jam. If it was a piece of cake or something nice, I would finish it off inside the entry before going out onto the street, so that I would not have to share it, not just because of my own greed, but the kids were always hungry and things like a piece of cake are hard to share with a bunch. Most of us were happy to get called in for tea and some of us would be out playing, including me, just to keep out of the way and to avoid being given jobs to do, but when in the winter months it would get cold and dark early and we had some cold winters in the Midlands during the '40s. Also it would get so dark people would nearly always carry a torch. Because of the war the lamplighter never came around to light up the street lights.

The only person who did come around was the Warden wearing his uniform and tin hat with a "W" on the front of it. He would thoroughly check every house for any speck of light showing through windows and doorways. All shop lights had to be out, greenhouses and factory glass roof lights had to be painted with whitewash so that if there was a moon it would not reflect a shine that would attract enemy aircraft. The rules were very strict on blackout.

The shops would stock blackout paper for people who only had thin or no curtains or other areas to cover. You would fix them up like a roller blind, tape them up by day and roll them down at night. The night wardens would be on duty all night doing a guard duty, checking the streets, doing policing, dealing with the odd drunk. He carried a police whistle. He would check out his local air raid shelters and make notes of any incidents that may occur or maintenance requiring attention like broken lampposts etc. (today's kids did not invent vandalism). All the time he would be on standby for an air raid because that's when most of them were and his job would have been to keep his head, stay calm and lead folks to a safe area, avoid panic if possible by his leadership and firmness.

They did a great job during the war and so did the people of the Midlands for keeping calm under fire and, contrary to belief, had their fair share of bombing raids. They kept working their arses off right through it keeping our industries going and knowing that our lives depended upon it and no mad upstart was going to change our way of life no matter how powerful he thought he was. Little Britain, Big Heart.

When in the house after being called in from play, I would have to wash my hands at the kitchen sink before sitting at the table with Mam and Alma. Alma would always glance over at my hands to make sure that they were suitably clean enough to be seated at the same table. I used to run straight in and to the table, but I soon learned that I would not get away with not being clean and tidy-ish at the meal table - and rightly so. My place was with my back to the back window. Alma would be seated on my right and Mam would sit on my left which was also handy for the kitchen door for Mam to co-ordinate the mealtime, especially on a Sunday, and Dad, when home, would sit opposite me facing the rear window. It was a rule in our home that all meals were taken at the dining table and together if possible. Tea and dinners would not be started until all were seated at the table except breakfast on weekdays and Dad often cooked the Sunday breakfast when home: good old fry up, yum.

On weekdays, after play, tea would be a simple affair that would often be home-made sandwiches and cake with a cup of tea. My cup of tea had milk and one small teaspoon of sugar stirred into it and I hated it, so I used to let it go cold and gulp it down in one as I was not allowed to leave the table until my plate was cleared and my tea cup was empty, except for the dregs i.e. tea leaves and tea powder that collected at the bottom of one's cup in those days. I would often swallow some of these in my haste to leave the table. When later in the year I was allowed out to play for a bit longer and always had to say 'please may I leave the table' after placing my eating irons together in a straight line pointing toward the centre of the table and would most times be asked to carry my plate into the kitchen to place ready for washing up, which was soon to become one of my chores.

Because Alma and I both had school dinners, Mam would have dinner at her place of work canteen, which was a small factory called the Black Cat, where they made ammunition. I think she was a capstan turner. She did not have to worry too much about us, but sometimes in the cold weather she would make a big pot of stew or soup and put it on the hotplate next to the open fire.

On those occasions, we would be allowed to huddle around the fire with a bowl of soup and often a pig's trotter for early supper and the living room fire was mostly the only heating in the house because of money and rationing.

Another reason we were allowed to have supper around the fire is that Mam would take over the table after tea, cover it with a big cloth and it would be her workbench for sewing, knitting, embroidery, wallpaper hanging, just name it, and she wasn't just average either, and Dad, woodwork, mechanic, gardening. Neither of them ever stopped making and creating. No wonder I love my work so much and don't ever want to retire.

The table was a typical square oak table with four solid corner legs with a low cross bar and a leaf which pulled out at each end to make the top larger. Ideal for those small terraced houses where the back room would be used as a living and dining room. My phobia for tea did not last too long as I learned that drinking it while still hot approaching warm wasn't too bad and that using a tea strainer was frowned upon by the people who know, as the tea continues to brew whilst in the cup and should be topped up with hot water if it becomes a bit strong for one's taste, plus the fact that you can't throw out the final drop of tea in order to read your future from the remaining tea leaves that are left in the cup, and my old Dad would not have a tea bag in his house right up until his dying day. It was always one for the pot, a little stir and give it two. Ha, he wouldn't have sliced bread either,

I am the same with bread and prefer a proper loaf, but I have succumbed to tea bags. The point I am really making is that I not only learned to like tea, it became my favourite drink from my early teens onwards and always my first thought in the morning.

11

In the warmer weather, Mam would pull out the table leaves to extend the table top to accommodate the extra dishes required for spreading out salad for self-service. We could eat as much as we wanted. Salad stuff and fresh veg did not last very long in the warm weather in the shops or the homes, as we did not have refrigerators or cold storage and most small shops would only have a very small ice cream freezer in those days. It was a case of what was available during the war. People would be queuing outside of shops even before they were open if they thought they were expecting a delivery or had one during the night or even heard a whisper – 'ha' and sometimes the queue would get bigger just because it was there.

A lot of our young women joined what was called The Land Army, run by the Government to supply a women's work force to help the War Effort by working on the land to help our farmers produce food to feed the nation. They were supplied with uniforms and kit, they were paid and treated the same as members of the armed forces and sent out to farms and postings all over the country to get billeted and fit in with farm life. It seemed that most of them enjoyed it, but they worked hard, and made a difference, as we needed all the local produce we could get. German U-boats were sinking so many of our ships coming home with food and supplies, far more than reported at the time. Some ships with important cargo would be escorted by the Royal Navy, which was also risky as a convoy would slow down a battle ship giving a bit more time for the German U-boats to form an ambush.

One reason why the odd merchant supply ship would get to port is because the Germans would be waiting for bigger fish like the above, and only have so many torpedoes, or didn't want it known that they were in the area, and more brownie points for a Royal Navy ship than a cargo ship. So we had to be as self-sufficient as we could be.

Mam was so good at organising and I didn't really know any better. I suppose her time in service helped her; she never got in a flap and was always saying this is what they do in the big houses when teaching me to clean the fire grate, the brasses, the silverware and dust the wooden furniture; that was my first chore. I remember seeing all the exotic bowls of mouth-watering fruit in the Tarzan films and more so in the old pirate films in technicolour: pineapples, grapes, bananas, etc. I had never seen or tasted most of these things but they looked great and we all used to shout out loud in the cinema Woow! even the grownups.

I finally got my first banana when I was 8 years old in 1945. Loved it. I will never forget the day that I smelt the skin of a banana that some lucky kid had thrown into the school playground rubbish box that used to hang from the wall in the bike shed like a flower box. It smelt nice and we all had a smell of it. Some lad had brought it back to school after going home for lunch (dinner). I couldn't wait to get home to tell my Mam. After school I ran all the way home (nothing new) and, as I rushed shouting and waving at Beauty, into the back door, I noticed a large fruit bowl on the kitchen prep table with apples, pears and topped with a big bunch of bananas.

She said, 'Have a glass of water, drink it slowly,' she was always telling me to drink water; then she said, 'You can go out to play with a piece of fruit,' laughing and knowing (one of those unforgettable moments in time). So, I went out on my street to show off and enjoy my first banana, only to be joined by two other kids with bananas.

Then my new friend, Peter Sparrow, joined me and I thought to share my banana with him. Peter and his family were very poor and he never had anything. Anyway, as I was finally beginning to unpeel my banana, my Mam opened our front door; then she beckoned Peter who went over to her wondering what he had done this time (he was always in trouble for something). Without fuss or ado, she just handed him a banana.

He said, 'Thank you Mrs Kent,' so politely. She smiled and shut the door. It made me happy. I was not sure that she would approve of him being a friend. She must have been watching us all through the window.

One never knew with my Mam which way she would go. So it was a good day all those years ago when Burton went bananas.

I didn't mind being called in early from play during the cold weather months, as it used to get dark early and sometimes wet or foggy or both. We always had a nice fire on in the living room that we would sit around after tea and listen to the wireless playing music and the news. At the end of the evening news they would read out secret messages in code for our undercover agents and units out in the field from the War Office and each other, including the odd fake message if they thought the Germans were on to the code to deliberately mislead them.

The Germans would also manage to get in with the odd message, like a game of cat and mouse using a double agent. I used to love listening about all of this stuff at Grandad's when the grown-ups would talk about the war. Mam would usually be at the table by now with her sewing machine or embroidery. Alma would often be knitting, whilst reading, whilst listening to the wireless, whilst getting her legs all blotchy from the heat of the fire by sitting too close to it. I would try a bit of knitting sometimes, but I used to hide it in case I got caught by a non-member of the family, so thought to be a bit girly. I did not mind doing some embroidery as I was told that my Dad liked doing it when he was in hospital recently and in his letter had said to tell me that in the next bed to him in this army hospital was a real Red Indian and that they were friends.

So darning and sewing was okay for men. I was quite good at darning and soon got to realise that if I was quiet and darning whilst listening to the wireless I would often get to stay up a bit later.

Most times Alma would pick me up on this and remind Mam that I had school in the morning so that I would get sent to bed. I would give her a bad look and she would smile. I wondered why she always did these things, but realised it was because she was a girl and thought she was grown-up. She was a pain most of the time, but we did have some good laughs together along the way, especially as I got older. She never lost that little streak about her and I always was aware that she had two sides, but I loved her always; she was my sister.

Going to bed was an ordeal in the winter, as the only warm room in the house would be the living room, so I would run up the stairs in my pyjamas and jump into my bed and curl up shaking and shivering with cold. As I warmed up I would slowly push my feet down the bed bit by bit. I remember that I used to pretend that I was tucked up in my lovely big bouncy pram outside...

Next thing I knew, I was being called to get up for school. I was never any problem getting up in the mornings, even when I didn't want to. I suppose I was well disciplined and have always understood orderly behaviour and teamwork and always liked to do for myself, like dressing and tying my own shoelaces. (Alma made me practise and practise that one before she would let me out to play when I was in her care on a Saturday when Mam was at work. This was so that she would not have to keep retying them on the way to school, as I did not tie them tight enough. She showed me how to do an extra knot and this stood me in good stead for when I joined the Cubs, and Scouts, for learning knot tying.

Alma was already a girl guide and I wanted to join, but Mam told me that I could join the Cubs next year, and I was happy with that and girls weren't allowed.

I was still happy at school and I don't think that my learning difficulties had been picked up on as yet. I had noticed that a few other kids in my year were having the same problem, so we were being segregated into separate groups for reading classes and my group were stuck on the old books whilst others were going onto new books with smaller printing and fewer pictures. This used to worry me because most of my group were not really bothered about school or learning anything and were bad at everything because they didn't care or want to learn, and some poor lambs were just backward children.

Even at this early age I knew that without reading and writing well, my learning would be slow and limited and that I had poor ability to concentrate on one thing at a time; yet in all other subjects that did not include reading and writing I would always hold my own; top with arts and crafts, in the gymnasium, and in the top three on the sports field.

After school, sometimes I would run all the way home and I remember wanting to time myself, but I never did as I couldn't tell the time either and I even had an old watch in my desk at school that cost me a set of fag cards, 100 unused cardboard milk tops and three taw marbles.

12

Tweedle-Dum has his day.

I came rushing home from school, as usual, one afternoon and, approaching our entrance gates that were mostly closed, as on this day, Peter Sparrow and Reggie Wallace, who were in the street, asked me if I was coming out to play and would I bring out my football for a kick about.

I said, 'Yes, hang on.'

So I collected the football from our scullery, then passed it to them through the wicket door of the big gates, telling them that I would join them soon as I needed the lavatory; so I doubled back and through our back gate and along our narrow yard to the WC.

Beauty would be watching me as she or he always did, as I never walked anywhere, and to a dog who has been chained up all day may have looked interesting. I would have already acknowledged him when stepping through the wicket door into the entry because he would start barking the minute he heard the latch click on the door. People in the street would jump and rush by the gates, especially if they were strangers, as his bark would echo so loudly when it hit the large brick entry; from outside he would sound like a wild beast.

If the car or trailer was not there, it would sound louder, which was good for us really and made us feel safer, so we would shout, "Hello Beauty!" and he would just wag his tail.

Anyway, after my Number 2 I would have pulled the chain that was hanging from a large wrought iron cistern that was fixed to the wall above the salt glazed white enamel pan, onto which was fixed a large hinged seat made of bare wood that got scrubbed regularly. So we were quite posh really in that we had a toilet that flushed direct from the water mains and proper mains drains. I didn't like using the sit-down toilets at school. They were a bit public and small in the juniors and I didn't like the small slippery toilet paper either. Much preferred screwed up newspaper, newsprint and all. Newspaper was very rough and bumpy in those days - a bit like a small version of wood chip wallpaper, and sometimes you couldn't read the words properly for bits of woodchip distorting the letters, and I couldn't read anyway, but it was good for wiping your bum with. There was no wash hand basin in the toilet, but most kids my age were not much into hygiene and neither were most grown-ups.

Anyhow, to get back on track and the main event of this story, I was now ready to go out on the street to play; so I opened the lav door (inwards) and stepped out whilst closing the door as I went, making sure that it was properly on latch as I was trained to do. It seems that I was so busy checking the latch that I did not notice someone was waiting in the yard for me; so as I turned to run down the yard, I froze, for there he was in all his glory. He must have been ten feet tall; his chest was out, his head was high and his wing span clouded any view beyond him.

I looked into his beady eyes that he kept closing, but I don't think he was winking. I knew that I would never get past him and that he was all fired up and ready to go and I knew that I wouldn't be able to shout him down or intimidate him like Dad would. He knew that I was just the little squirt that lived in the house –and teased him – sometimes.

So, after weighing up the pros and cons and noticing that he was already in the starting blocks and sure wouldn't give me time to get back into the toilet to do the Number 3 I now needed, the only thing left to do was leg it away from him (all this thinking and planning must have been one of the longest split seconds of my life).

So I started to run away from him screaming, 'Mam!' I ran toward the shed but that was closed and I had no time to open the door and he was right behind me. I had to get out of that corner, so I pushed off the shed as Dum crashed into it; then I jumped up onto the stone slab top, which was a bad move, but when I bounced from the shed I didn't know that Dum was going to hit the shed or even where he was, so I could have run down to the house where my Mam was already outside with the sweeping brush. But now Dum had joined me on the slab - he just got up there in one jump; then he pecked me a couple of times as I was scrambling down. Next thing I was running down the yard with Dum hanging on the back of my trousers. I was shouting and screaming; the other chickens were creating; Beauty was barking and jumping up and down.

I reached Mam and she pushed Dum off me with the sweeping brush whilst I shot in through the kitchen door and went into the living room to look out of the rear window to see her walk past Dum, up to the chicken pen, followed by Dum. She opened the pen wire framed door and he scampered in squawking and beating his wings. Then Mam strolled back to the house, smiling and pointing at all the feathers everywhere. She entered the house and we all fell about laughing.

'That served you right,' she said. I nodded my head with agreement. As I was laughing with her and Aunty May, Alma arrived home from school and joined in the laugh. She was sorry to have missed it, so it was all great fun really. I wasn't hurt, just a couple of pecks. We never did find out how he got out, but the way he'd come up to me on that slab, I reckon that he could get over the top of the pen any time he wanted to. And although that was the first, it was not the last time that he was to chase me down the yard. But all the other times he was to chase me, I used to love it and ran from him, laughing so much that he would catch up with me sometimes. It was like a game as he never ever chased anyone else.

So, after the great escape, I could now go out to play. When I got into the street there were about four of us now and my turn in goal after showing my injuries and explaining all the commotion that could be heard in the street from our yard. They thought it was good fun. Then we had a kick about. The goal posts were chalked out on the long high wall that ran from No. 1 Dale Street to Cracker

Law's barber shop. Also chalked out were cricket stumps, and hopscotch was usually chalked out on the wide section of pavement outside the Ballinger family house opposite the wall. Also the Ballingers had lots of girls in their family.

Ours was a good street for playing in and other kids used to come from the side streets as Dale Street was a long and wide-ish one (for its day), that joined onto a main road at each end with four local shops, a pub and off-licence, a dairy and ten minutes walk to the town centre. By late afternoon it would be rare to see more than the odd car or horse and cart. They all drove slowly in the streets and a horse always had right of way, plus all road users knew there were always kids playing on the streets and nobody minded. It was a way of life then - not the rat race of the roads today. People loved the horses and used to give them tit-bits after getting permission from the driver, unless he was in the pub, and the horses knew this and was probably another reason why they were so friendly with the kids and street people.

My football was given to me by John Leedham, our neighbour's son. It was a really old leather original lace-up. The leather was so thin and worn that when you gave it a good kick, it would make a sound like a kettle drum and fly up in the air like a balloon, and I used to put dubbin on it to make it look better and give it more weight. Jack Leedham used to give me pigs' bladders to put inside the ball to blow up and tie before lacing up the leather case. It was quite common practice in the old days to use a pig's bladder in a football and my mates and I were very grateful.

I also remember a couple of times he gave me a bag of bones saying, 'Take these bones, there's a couple of marrow bones in there with meat on for your dog and the others you and your mates can make clappers out of.'

I knew what he meant because I had seen chaps playing them in the pub and some of the big lads at school with them, so I told Mam, who gave Betty, our Manchester Terrier, both of her bones that had some raw meat still on them. Then she sorted out the best suitable clapper bones for me. They all looked pretty flat to me - I suppose they were rib bones - I don't know. I guess the best ones in those days would have been ivory.

Mam told me to share the rest with my friends, first come, first served, so that's what I did, and they decided to get round the tinker man when he came down the street next time to see if he would shape them up a bit. I asked my Mam if I could use a couple of

Dad's tools. She said "no" as I knew she would. He had a great set of tools and was very good with them. I had seen him finishing off things with a rasp and a file and thought they would do the job on my clappers. I loved to watch him work with his tools; he would have been a wonderful craftsman with proper training. But I was given a "no" on the tools and from my parents "no" was 'no'. Then I remembered watching my Dad sharpening knives, so Peter Sparrow and I shaped our clappers on the big sandstone slab at the end of our garden.

The next significant thing that happened to me was probably one of the most traumatic things that ever happened. I was sitting in front of the living room fire with Mam. Alma wasn't home; maybe she wasn't supposed to be, when Dad turned up, unexpected to me, and Mam and Dad had this terrible row. Dad wasn't saying much. Mam was shouting at him. I was sobbing; I had never seen my parents like this before. Mam told Dad to get out and never come back and Dad walked out of the back door wearing his army uniform.

I was crying loudly now because I was scared and panic stricken.

Mam grabbed hold of me and started to cry herself. I didn't understand what was happening and I remember her saying, 'Promise that you will never leave your Mam.' and I promised her that I would never leave her and always look after her (big deal I was not even seven years old yet) and I was worried about my Dad whom I loved so much.

I was too young to understand what was going on and I never did know. Alma once told me that Dad had a fling with a school mistress whilst in the army, but that is all I ever remember of that incident. But that night had a profound effect upon me for the rest of my life.

The year of '43 is closing in now. My schoolwork is poor but I don't worry about it much. I look forward to dinner time and home time. I don't play out much at the moment as it is cold and dark early evenings and I am beginning to enjoy the wireless with the live shows, music, stories, some of the news and messages.

War update:
Surrender at Stalingrad marks Germany's first major defeat.

Allied victory in North Africa enables invasion of Italy to be launched.

Italy surrenders, but Germany takes over the battle.

British and Indian forces fight Japanese in Burma.

Christmas came and went. I don't remember much of it, but it would have been a good one - they always were with our family and friends, especially during the war. I don't remember any mention of Dad during Christmas and New Year, not in front of me anyway, and I did not ask any questions as I knew it was a sensitive subject. In those days children were supposed to be seen and not heard. The situation was still bothering me, however. He was my Dad, my hero, and at war.

13

It is now January 1944 and I am back at school after the winter holidays. Same school but have moved up into the juniors (not by merit but age). It is adjacent to the infants' school but bigger with a large playground.

We were lined up in the playground in a similar fashion as to what we were taught in the infants' school but more disciplined and quietly after the whistle or bell had gone. Everything was done in a military fashion and was good for health and safety and the War Effort, and the truth is that we children enjoyed playing little soldiers in the playground carrying our gas masks, and we all knew exactly what to do, not if, but when there were air raids, fires or other emergencies.

After being shuffled into one file with the shortest at the front and the tallest at the back, we were marched single file into the school and into a classroom where a teacher would tell us where to sit starting at the front desks and working back into the classroom until all the children were seated.

The teacher who took charge looked like an elderly man of about fortyish, told us all to be quiet, then introduced himself and his young assistant who was by now dishing out new exercise books one to each child. The assistant was a young girl student teacher who would also work with the other teachers in the school as and when needed. There were about twenty-five of us in the class, most of whom I knew as they had come up with me from last year's term. Some had come from other schools; some were new to Burton including a couple of evacuees.

My desk was on the left wall side, second row in from the front and we were told that these would be our regular seats and that this would be our own classroom for the full term, although we would be using other classrooms and teachers for some lessons. The desks were the normal structure of those days: solid oak tops with a lid fixed to a heavy wrought iron framework to which was also fixed a solid oak seat. These were mostly made in pairs and they were very heavy (not very nick–able).

Trouble is it was a mixed school and I got to sit with a girl, but I didn't mind too much because I had just avoided being on the front desks and we were next to a wall with a large window above for light and she was happy because there was one of those massive cast iron radiators on the wall next to her and it was cold weather. I also remembered her from last term; she was always clean and tidy and spoke nicely. We actually became good pals and she used to help me with some of my school work.

As the days went by, I realised how lucky we were in my class to have such a great teacher. We all loved him; he was such a character - he was an old sea dog. I can't remember his name, probably because we all called him Captain behind his back and Sir to his face. He had been in the Navy and was always talking about ships and naval history, of which he knew a lot and his geography was top hole. He was to be my main teacher for a couple of years and we were to become good pals.

I developed a high regard for him and always worked hard in his class, which wasn't difficult as he always made his lessons so interesting and made us feel comfortable. When he wanted to be strict, you knew not to play up; even the other teachers seemed to look up to him. I am sorry that he wasn't my teacher for Maths, English, and the other academic stuff that I was useless at.

I remember the old Captain used to do story time for us a couple of times a week and they were great. We would come charging in from the playground the second the bell started to ring. We would rush to our seats and sit up straight as we did not want to miss one minute of story time. That was usually the last lesson of the day following playtime, so there was no time wasted calling out the register and then it was home time afterwards. Oh, what a lovely life.

Then the old Captain walked in from the end door of the classroom, through the aisle and sat at his desk, opened the lid and took out a large hardback book that had *Charles Dickens* on the front. He put the book on the desk and, after he put his glasses on, he would lay a hand on his book, smirk, and say, 'Where were we?' and we would all shout something like:

"Bill Sikes has just killed Nancy and Patch his dog has run out the door".

Even the assistant teacher would join in as she used to love his story telling. He would do all the accents; he would jump up from his desk and go into character and walk up and down doing Bill Sikes and Fagin. He didn't need the book as he knew all the lines like a script. His Long John Silver from *Treasure Island* was a treasure itself with the classroom sweeping brush under his arm and a chalk duster on his shoulder pretending to be a parrot that would fall off, and he would ask one of the kids to pick up his parrot and put it back on his shoulder as it couldn't fly and he couldn't pick it up because of his wooden leg. His stories were a real treat; he would make us laugh, cry, sad, happy, scared, pantomime and the end of story time lesson would be over as the last school bell of the day rang out. None of us rushed out of the door after we were dismissed like on a normal class; we always wanted to know what happened next, but were told that we would have to wait until the next story time, and we all went home happy. I think that the old Captain enjoyed story times as much as we did and what a great way to teach kids the old classics. I reckon that we learned a lot more on those fun lessons than we realised and that is why I still remember them so vividly.

I liked going to school but my reading and writing were holding me back on everything else. For instance: we were now learning to write with pen and ink - that was a metal pen nib pushed into a metal collar holder which was fitted tightly around a wooden stem making the whole pen about six inches long and a quarter inch diameter. You had to dip the nib into a small ink pot about the size of an egg cup and this was fitted into a hole at the top of each desk and called an ink well. I found it very difficult   using these pens mainly because I am left handed and they wanted you to slant your letters slightly to the right and, as English goes from left to right, means that you are smudging your work with your pen hand as you go, so your blotting paper also gets wet. Because this slows you down you don't get time to take in the information that you are writing about or the class discussion after it, as you are still writing yours down after the rest have finished.

This was very demoralising for me, especially in later years when the teacher would be using two blackboards. When getting to the end of the second board the teacher would rub out the first board in order to continue. I wasn't the only one in class to suffer this way; there were two or three of us, but we didn't complain as we considered it to be our own fault for not paying attention and being backward, but the teachers knew who we were because our books were left for marking. I suppose, in fairness, the teachers had their end of term standards to achieve and to encourage their best pupils in their subjects. Ballpoint pens would have been better but they hadn't been invented yet and they used to smudge quite a lot when they first came out. Even a nice fountain pen was not allowed to be used in school. Looking back, I think left handers and slow writers should have been allowed to use pencils when copying a volume of work that had to be retained for reference and notes regarding further lessons. They could always be copied over in ink but at least you would have your notes. That was always discouraging in the next lessons not having references and having to blag your way through a lesson, so you felt bad about yourself and slid back even more.

Before I leave this boring subject I must say how much I have always loved the old scroll writings, all done with a feather quill - and the writings still done by monks with patterns done around leading letters and the edges of books often added with real gold and silver water gilding. It is the ultimate in signwriting; it is soothing and hypnotic to watch, even on film, (and not rushed by the way).

After school I would play in the street. I was allowed out after tea which was normally about 5pm and had to come in doors at 7pm. Sometimes, if play was not good, or wet or cold, I would go in at 6:45, in time to hear *Dick Barton, Special Agent*, with his two comrades, Jock and Snowy. It was on every week night for fifteen minutes and always ended on a cliffhanger. All five episodes were repeated in one go on Saturday morning, so you could catch up then if you wanted to. It was a popular show and I enjoyed it at the time. I can even remember the signature tune it was called *The Devil's Gallop*, and it went like Dun drun dun drun dun drun dun dun dun dun dun dundun daaaaaaaa. Get it? We all used to shout the DB theme when playing cops and robbers. But my favourite tune was still *Over the Rainbow*.

Mam was still working at the black cat factory on night shift making ammo for the war. On Friday nights Alma's friends used to come round to our house for the evening, as Alma had to look after me and sometimes one or two of them would sleep over. Trouble was Friday night was bath night for me, which meant that the boiler would be stoked up and the tin bath was placed on the kitchen floor and Alma was supposed to bathe me, but by the time she'd had her bath and dressed, her mates were arriving and I was getting my bath. The door between the kitchen and living room kept opening and closing and the girls were giggling and shouting "can I help?" and other things and giggling more. I really did not mind the girls; they liked me and we all got on well and when they were around the house was always happy. In fact, I did let them bathe me sometimes and I would wear my swim pants. Then I would sit with them for a while until Alma sent me off to bed.

Sometimes I would creep down the stairs and peep through the door and listen to them talking and giggling. They were aged between eleven and thirteen and most of it was about boys and not going over my head.

Next thing I was waking up with two girls in my bed because I had the big front room with a double bed. This happened many times and I was okay with it. Aunties, Uncles friends, cousins – it was the normal thing in those days.

14

The next thing I remember is my birthday. It was March 7th 1944 and I was seven years old and spoiled as usual. I had a Hornby train set pack with carriages and interlocking assembly track that could be extended (and was buying extra pieces later). I loved it and had it for years. Apparently my great-grandfather on my Mam's side was a steam engine driver for the Great Western Railways at Burton; his surname was Andrews.

I also had a new small child violin complete with case, bow and rosin. My Grandad Skivington was going to teach me how to play and read music, as he was a brilliant player and already teaching my cousin, Derick, who was seven years older than me. I was still not allowed to even sit at the piano and Alma locked the lid. Once Mam left the front door open to let some air flow through the house - quite common in those days - folks would never steal from each other, but that did not mean that their kids, my mates, would not run in, tinkle out a couple of notes, then run off laughing, giving Alma an excuse to lock the lid. It used to stand against the wall between the front door and the middle door.

It was a good birthday. I was chuffed with my pressies and cards. I remember a white card with a big red number seven on it, but not the others. I suppose it was prominent and easy to memorise.

My next memory was of my Uncle Charlie coming over to see Mam. He was her youngest brother and her favourite. I liked him too and he was a good singer who sounded like Nat King Cole. He had his son with him who stayed over for a week whilst his Dad went back to Long Eaton just outside of Burton, where he worked as a coalminer. I think it was the Easter break and Uncle Charlie was splitting up with his wife at the time.

They also had a little girl who was with her Mum. The children were twins; I can't remember their names and I don't think I ever met his first wife or the girl. I only met the boy once more after his stay with us and cannot remember his name either. I think it was John. But we got on really well; it was like having a little brother. He was a bit younger than me but we had fun and I shall always remember his ambition was to have false teeth like his Dad so that he could just put them into a glass of water at night. He loved his Dad, who didn't, his wife maybe? I was sorry when he went back home. I only ever saw him once shortly after that.

It was around this time that I arrived home from school to notice an American jeep in our street, parked outside of our house and that our front door was open. Not seeing anyone, I still went in the back way as always to say hello to Beauty, plus I was not allowed to run in and out of the front door. As I went into the back door, I noticed Mam sitting at the table with a couple of Americans who were wearing military uniforms. They were drinking tea or coffee and on the table there were tins of powdered drinking chocolate, powdered milk, peanuts, chewing gum and silk stockings.

Mam said to me, 'Say hello to Joe and his friend,' whose name I probably forgot there and then. I said 'hello' and he said 'Hi' and shook my hand; then Mam said to me, 'You may go out to play with your friends for a while,' in her posh embarrassing tone that she would use sometimes, just like Alma.

Joe butted in whilst I was changing my shoes in the kitchen, and Mam called me back into the living room where Joe passed me a big bag of sweets saying, 'Share these with your friends.'

I looked at my Mam as I said thank you to Joe. She had a smiling approval look on her face; she knew that I had never seen so many sweets in one go, only in a shop window, and sweets were considered a luxury and on ration so you weren't allowed many even if you had the money, which we didn't. I thought to myself, I like these guys and went running out to play with my spoils where my street pals had started to gather around the jeep. And when I produced my big bag of sweets, it was party time.

It wasn't long before they came out, jumped into their jeep, drove to the next corner, Paget Street, turned around and drove back down Dale Street, throwing packs of chewing gum at us kids, waving and tooting their horn.

Mam was at the front door laughing. She loved anyone with a bit of front and the "Yanks" as we called them then seemed a bit brash compared to the British more reserved way of life. So that was my first of many meetings with Joe and his pal. Joe was a good-looking chap - looked a bit like Errol Flynn, the film actor, and had a small moustache. I think he was an officer and his buddy was his driver as he had stripes and wore a different hat, whereas Joe had a round peak hat and stuff on his epaulets (shoulder straps).

We had been getting a few air raids around this time and, although London got really blitzed, we did take some hammering in the Midlands where most of our industrial factories were. They were busy producing stuff for the war in secret, to be transported in sections, to be assembled by a chosen few who would know what the parts were for, and then taken to their chosen site, like model planes, tanks, transport, buildings, etc. Also real wooden large glider planes capable of carrying a troop of men with their fighting equipment, and other big items in preparation for D-Day. It was a massive undertaking and just proved what this little island is capable of when its people are up against it.

You have to admit that the whole strategy smelled of British humour, and that is probably why the Jerries could not figure out what we were up to. They knew we were up to something, and we knew that they knew, so we kept misleading them by playing the daisy chain like *'The Man Who Never Was'*, but that's all been covered by a better author than me.

I was walking to school one morning, after one of these night raids and, as I looked over the road on Uxbridge Street, the house where one of my school mates lived was missing, and there were a couple of men with a handcart clearing the area and no one was allowed to walk on that side of the road. There was also a policeman and an air-raid warden there. When I arrived at school my school friend was already there in the playground surrounded by lots of new friends. Apparently he had wanted to come into school anyway and it was probably the best place for him, as his mum had to see the welfare people. He was to go to his grandparents after school and they lived just over the road from school. It seemed that no one was hurt as they were all in the dug-out shelters in the Christ Church rear plot of land. We went to the brick built shelter on Meller's garden on Dale Street that night.

When I got home from school in the afternoon (walking for a change), I was surprised to see that the bombed site had been cleared and workmen were fixing large wooden beams between the two buildings either side of the missing house; this fascinated me and I seemed to understand exactly how and why they were doing this in a certain way. So it was my first experience of a building being shored up. The shoring took a couple of days to complete but it was made safe by that evening, and the families either side were allowed back in after a couple of days.

I often used to look at the bombed site when passing and remember how strange it looked with the fire places still there and the wallpaper being exposed with no roof or floors and admiring the way the timber shoring was done, not realising that I would be doing some myself in years to come. The gap between the remaining houses was not filled in or built on up to when I moved to live in a different area of Burton about four years later after the war; so I don't know what happened to the gap. I seem to remember that it was fenced off and a large advertising hoarding board was put up on the plot.

We were often mistaken for Leicester, Coventry and Derby, plus we had some massive breweries in Burton that would look like large factories from the air as they were often hit, causing loss of lives.

My next nice memory is the evening I shook hands with the great "Tommy Handley" who was one of Britain's greatest showbiz personalities during the war. He was very popular and used to head the top radio show called I.T.M.A. *It's That Man Again.* The format would consist of this quick-witted comedian who would wander around meeting and bumping into different people from all walks of life and played by character actors who all had their own catchphrases. They all became very famous during and after the war, like John Pertwee who was better remembered for *Wurzel Gummage* and *Doctor Who*.

Anyway, Mam got two tickets for a live show of I.T.M.A. with the complete cast and the Stanley Black orchestra at one of our local cinemas, of which we had three. It was the one near the Burton Railway station and I think it was called the Odeon.

So we went to the show and we were at the front which was great and I understood it more than the radio because it was a fast and quick witted show. Because I was so young I didn't get all the jokes, but because they used all of these silly voices and catch phrases that were known and used all over the country like, "Can I do you now sir?" by Mrs Mopp, and "It's being so cheerful that keeps me going" after having a good moan about something. And "Don't forget the diver", "T.T.F.N." a dog called Upsey being told to get down, and end up being up-downsy. A lot of the voices were done by a man called Jack Train who was our most famous impressionist and was in great demand in radio days. He knew how to use a mike to sound like anything; he wasn't called Train for nothing. I suppose the show was a bit like an early kind of goon show - silly but clever and topical.

So as the show ended, and we all stood up for the King, Mam noticed that two ushers were opening the end side door that was situated next to the stage, or usually the screen, all but a gangway between. The other side of the door was a small foyer with a kiosk where we would normally pay and enter for the cheap seats called the stalls for the cinema, but in this case, they were the best seats.

As they were taking their final bow, Mam noticed that Tommy was wearing a white silk scarf and put two and two together. Tommy waved to the audience from middle stage; he then went to the back of the rest of the cast and, because we were at the front, saw him come down the steps from the stage to the exit door.

Mam had already clocked it. As he was coming down the steps of the stage, she was grabbing my hand and saying "come on". So I went, not being too sure what was going on. But what Mam said was okay with me and I only remember this bit because I heard the story repeated many times by her, but the rest I can remember like it was yesterday.

We pushed through the staff at the door, who were trying to hold it for the cast only and lead the audience out through the main front entrance. Anyway, Mam and I were hard on the heels of Tommy who had now reached the end of the alleyway that ran the length of the theatre to the front street. When we caught up with him, he was about to get into a car that was ready and waiting, and was in the process of opening the car door himself as his driver had the engine running, when my Mam said to him, 'Tommy, will you shake hands with my son?'

He said, 'Of course,' and gave me a proper good handshake and clasped his other hand over as he asked me direct, 'What is your name?'

I said, 'Gordon,' and he said to me, 'Gordon, you look after your Mum, yes?' as if I was talking to one of my favourite uncles. Then he stroked my Mam's arm as he was getting into his car. He wound down the window and said to her, 'I must go,' as he had to be in some place that night and the people were now starting to come out of the front of the theatre.

Tommy then said to Mam, 'If you hang about you will be able to get Stanley Blacks' autograph.' Then he shouted as they drove off: 'He will be the one pushing a wheelbarrow full of money!'

Mam started to laugh out loud as they waved goodbye. By now, people were herding out of the picture house, most of them going to their homes, talking to each other in silly voices and using all of the catch phrases and singing the "It's that man again" signature tune.

A few were hanging on for autographs. A lady came up to us and asked us who was in the car waving; she was one of the first out and when Mam said it was Tommy Handley, she said, 'I thought it was.'

Mam said, 'He shook hands with my son,' and the woman said, 'You lucky boy.' Then she shouted to the others that Tommy had already left.

They didn't believe us and were saying things like, "Where's your autograph then?"

Mam said, 'Instead of hanging around we will walk home with a bag of chips each. After all, we got to the show, and got to talk and shake the hand of the great man himself, Tommy Handley. You will never forget this night.' (You were right, Mam. Thanks to your good spirit and pushiness).

At the time I didn't understand the joke that Tommy had shouted out to Mam, so she explained to me on the way that Stanley

Black, who was one of our most famous orchestra and band leaders in the country, during and after the war, would get the biggest pay packet because he would have to also pay his top musicians of the band, and would need a wheelbarrow to carry it all. But it took me years to pick up all the innuendoes of the joke, like Stanley Black having a liking for money and a bargain, and other good-humoured banter between them.

15

It was about a year since the great *Dambusters* raid on the German river Rhine, breaching their two main dams with the newly invented bouncing bomb, causing flooding to the Ruhr valley where they had important arms factories and putting them out of action, on the 16th and 17th of May 1943.

Whether this was a successful operation or not, due to heavy flak going into and out of Germany, costing the lives of many good men and aircraft, it did inspire the British people with its daring and imagination and "never say never" arrogance that had won us the day so many times.

For the past twelve months our factories had been going flat out for the War Effort. Mam was working overtime and night shifts. Poor Alma had to stay home to look after me (no wonder she hated me). Anyway, she didn't look after me as much as Mam thought and I was allowed to run riot most of the time, even to the point of being locked out, but that didn't bother me until I got hungry.

We still made regular visits to Grandma's; Aunty Evelyn was living there at the time with her two children: my cousins, Prunella and Billy Boy. They were posted back home from India where they had married quarters with her husband, my Uncle Bill. Billy Boy was born over there and was just a child – they were to have two more children. We were always a very close family and they were like brothers and sisters to me.

One weekend when we visited, Uncle Bill was there and the women were sewing some new stripes on the uniform sleeves of his BD battle dress tunic, denim tops and arms of his greatcoat. The Americans loved our greatcoats and would give just about anything to get hold of one, as they were so warm and great to wear on a cold night, especially on guard duty.

At the top of the sleeves on each arm, a British soldier would wear what was called a flash; that was normally a piece of embroidered material about two inches square with a motif or logo signifying what command you were attached to. This would be sewn onto the top side of each arm of your tunic that you were wearing.

Although my Uncle Bill had joined up with the Royal Artillery, same as his elder brother (my Dad), the flash that was to go on his tunic was *Airborne Division* and it was a new motif. I loved it as it was a sky-blue *Pegasus* on a dark red background. I managed to get hold of one, as we kids all collected war bits and pieces.

It seemed that Uncle Bill was training to fly gliders, which he did very soon. Pru was growing up and I could remember her as a smaller child. Little Billy had been given the name my Mam wanted to call me, but she changed it after her younger sister, Edie, married Uncle Bill and stated that she would call her first son Bill after his Dad. So what's in a name anyhow?

Billy Boy and I grew to be great chums, and he grew up to have his own army career and retired as a Colonel with a MBE from the Queen, who said to him "Well done, Billy and so say all of us".

His father, RSM Bill Kent, would have been so proud to have called him "Sir" – with a salute each way.

I saw a fair bit of Joe (Mam's American friend) around this time, but they were not in my face and I never saw anything untoward. Mam was always happy when he was around, so that was okay with me and I was always getting goodies to share with my mates. I did pick up on a couple of snide remarks by a nosey neighbour who wouldn't have known the circumstances anyway and would not dare confront my Mam.

I think she was a bit mad; she always wore the same clothes, never went out and I was told that newspapers were strewn all over her floors. She used to hang around her doorway or peeping through her curtains. She hated us kids and used to tell us to clear off. When it started getting dark early, we would knock on her door and run away. Once we tied a piece of cotton to her door knocker then hid behind the side wall, giggling as we pulled the cotton to knock the door. Then when she opened the door we ran away laughing out loud.

She knew who we were and I think she half enjoyed the attention, as I often saw her laughing at us as we played in the street. I think we were all a bit mad in those days.

My next memory of this time was when I arrived home from school or in from play and Joe's jeep was outside. As I went in, I saw Mam, Alma and Joe with his buddy, both in uniform. They were all looking sad and Mam said to me say goodbye to Joe and Buddy they had to go away.

They both shook hands with me and then Joe gave me a ten-bob note. I couldn't believe it; I had never touched that much before. It was enough to buy a good pair of shoes or, even better, 120 ice creams in a cornet. Then I went over to Alma who was standing near the kitchen door whilst Mam said her goodbyes near the middle doorway to the front room and door.

I said to Alma, 'Look what Joe gave me,' flashing my lovely ten-shilling note, and she said to me, 'He gave me One Pound,' showing me her £1 note and whispered, 'That's because he loves me twice as much as you.'

That was it. I was off again wailing and crying.

Mam came over and said, 'What is the matter?' and I tried to explain badly.

Meanwhile, Joe had put two and two together, made five and was trying to hand another ten-bob note to Mam to give to me, to which she rightly said, 'No Joe. He has quite enough,' and it got left at that.

No one understood that I was just being touchy; it was nothing to do with the money. I was more than chuffed with ten shillings. It was just that after Alma pushed my buttons, I realised that had I not turned up when I did, I would have missed their farewell altogether as it was only a fleeting visit to say goodbye.

They were going straight off on manoeuvres and didn't know where, so off they went never to be seen again.

I have to smile when I look back. My sister had the wickedest sense of humour I have ever known and could play me better than she could play her damned piano.

The town was very busy; there was lots of transport about and the factories were all going flat out for the War Effort. People were talking of a German invasion. We kids were always talking about the Germans coming to get us and what they would do to us and made up stories to scare each other and ourselves. Most of our stories were an exaggeration of listening in on the grown-up's chatter, but there were always stories going around that they could be here tomorrow, and it was always a genuine shared fear.

So, it was now the morning of Tuesday 6th June 1944. And it was said that there was an air of quiet about the town. The factories were all working full tilt as usual, but the roads seemed empty and people were looking at each other quizzically. There was a sense of "What?"

Then the news came over the wireless that thousands of our troops: British, American, Canadian, under the command of General Eisenhower were landing and pushing forwards under heavy fire. They were at

Normandy in Northern France in order to liberate France and its people, including the Channel Islands, and to give us access into Europe. Our troops were taking in tanks, lorries, jeeps, artillery including field guns, even tents and maybe a kitchen sink. The operation was set off by an advance party of paratroopers and the SAS, including a load of dummy ones, that were dropped off over a different area to mislead the Germans. There were many brave lads in the gliders nicknamed "flying coffins", and ongoing cover fire from our massive fleet of ships. Our aircraft outnumbered the Luftwaffe thirty to one.

The BBC were giving out hourly reports and our people were loving it as we'd had a hammering and felt like we had been placed to one side to be dealt with later. But now we were not the underdogs and the worm had turned.

So, the taking and liberation of France was ongoing, and I suppose that is why Joe and Buddy went off in a hurry. I never heard any more of them, but I hoped that they got through the war okay; they were good guys.

I think Uncle Bill went in with Pegasus Sixth Airborne horse gliders and he would have stayed there because those gliders only landed once and there was no way back. I believe he was a despatch rider as I remember this one story I heard of him at one of the family meetings. He was delivering despatches one dark night between lines with lots of firing going on, when a German helmet landed on his lap as he was riding his motorbike and had to stop to remove it, as it was wedged in and too heavy to flick off. As he lifted it from his lap, he was surprised that it was so heavy. As he was wondering whether to keep it, there was more shell fire that lit up the sky and Uncle Bill noticed this Germans face staring at him from inside his helmet. Uncle Bill let out a shriek, threw the head and helmet down and sped off to do his job.

I didn't know where my Dad was at this time as he was still not spoken of in front of me, but I worried about him in the war. Although I hadn't seen much of him in my short life, I knew he was a good man and he was my Dad. I don't know if he was involved in the Normandy Landings or not, but there was also a story about my Dad, who would only talk about good things when he did talk, which was rare.

I think it was about this time that my Dad was in charge of a gun crew on the French borders and had a lone gun and a crew dug out and camouflaged at a strategic point overlooking some open fields. One day the Battery Commander came over to see how they were coping, bringing some dry rations with him like tea, coffee, dried milk saying, 'Sorry Tom, but we haven't had any supplies from HQ for days. But I managed to bring you a couple of chickens for now.'

Tom (Dad) said back, 'Oh thank you, Sir. Well just hang them up with the others.'

'What others?' said Sir, following Dad into a dug out behind the gun with a supported roof and props taken from the nearby woods just like in the coal pits. Hanging in there were chickens, rabbits, best part of a pig, and vegetables, and Sir went back to Battery camp with loads of bacon, eggs, and a couple of rabbits. He said, 'No wonder your men are loyal,' smiling.

Dad was a good cook, and being raised on a smallholding and, with his experience of farm work and the land, was a natural survivor. He would have been in his element looking after his crew.

One day, Dad and a couple of his crew were walking along one of the fields not far from the Gun Post, looking for mushrooms plus whatever else was in the offing, and they were staying close to the hedge as always to keep a low profile. This hedge was in a larger field and cornered off at a right angle. My

Dad and his two mates in uniform were armed with loaded rifles (you never went anywhere without your rifle, even on leave) so they were coming close to the corner of the hedge now. But so too were three German soldiers in uniform and bearing firearms on the other side of the fence. Oh my God, they came face to face; the earth stood still for a split second, but then with such lightning speed, as if on automatic impulse – yes, you're right, they all turned and ran away from each other. Probably shrieking like girls.

I always loved that story. Just shows that normal people don't want to run around killing each other given a choice. Makes one wonder who the real enemies are.

People seemed more cheered up now and we were getting regular updates of the biggest invasion in history over the following days and weeks. We were also worried about our troops, as losses would be great and many would not come home, but it seemed necessary in order to gain access into Europe and free the French who would join us. It was also necessary to get the German U-boats out of the English Channel as they were putting a stranglehold on us by sinking our ships with supplies and people coming in and going out.

It felt like our first real fight back and it felt extra good because we were still licking our wounds from Dunkirk, in May 1940. That was when we were driven out of France by the Germans with great loss of life during the evacuation on the beaches and at sea. The Dunkirk exodus also showed what a great little nation the Brits are. When in trouble they roll up their sleeves, close ranks and spill guts.

16

Summer of '44 was fun. School was okay; I quite liked it. I just wasn't any good at stuff like education.

The old Captain had noticed that I liked drawing, so he called me over to his desk one day, as we were filing out of the classroom, and showed me a picture of a sailing ship in a book. It was the Santa Maria in colour on a shiny page.

He said to me, 'Could you copy this in coloured chalks on my blackboard for tomorrow afternoon's history lesson?' and I said yes.

He normally did them himself and I always thought that they were a bit rubbish. I knew I could do better, especially at copying as I was okay at getting the proportions right when enlarging or reducing the size. In those days I was better at copying than using my imagination, especially with animals.

We agreed that I would draw it during the dinner break and try to get it finished for the lesson, which I did. I used up a whole blackboard (one of the upright sliding types). The old Captain was chuffed and said jokingly, 'I will tell everyone that I did it.'

We both laughed. I was pleased that he liked it as I had a lot of respect for him, plus I was happy with it; it was the biggest thing I had ever drawn, and it looked better from a distance. When the class came in, they were surprised, and I got a round of applause. This was to be the first of many.

I sat down at my desk with my girl mate, Chris, to enjoy a history lesson about the Spanish Armada, whilst picking out my faults in my masterpiece - as we artists do – ha!

I went on to do many others for the old Captain, including: the Vikings, Golden Hind, the Victory, Clipper, Roman Ships, Modern Ships, a few planes and trains like Stevenson's Rocket. The Captain loved his old ships. I enjoyed doing them and did not mind giving up some playtime sometimes, or during a free lesson or art lesson when our classroom was empty. It gave me a bit of attention of the right sort, helped me with my confidence and, looking back, I think the old sea dog realised these things and that I struggled with concentration.

He was a gifted teacher and seemed to know how to bring the best out of everyone, but I will always remember him most for his storytelling with his actions and voices; pure magic.

On the way home from school I would sometimes stop off en route at one of my mates' houses. The school was close to Grandma's house on Broadway Street and Auntie Tess on Napier Street, where my cousins, Derek - who was fifteen and Terry - who was nine, lived. I often called in on them. Derek was in the Navy Cadets. I had plenty of friends and relations between home and around my school area. I took myself to school now, so was allowed to run around more and stay out later in the light nights. I had a cooked school dinner every weekday which meant that tea in the summer would be sandwiches or salad or something that would be placed to one side to eat when I got in. The only day of the week that we seemed to eat together was on a Sunday, as Mam was doing night shifts at the ammunition factory whilst Alma took care of my tea, welfare, bedtime and up for school. Alma and I had an understanding that I would rush in after school and gobble my tea as quickly as possible without having to share my table manners, then shoot out to play without popping in and out, so that she could get on with her schoolwork, reading, friends, or latest boyfriend.

She would say, 'If you pop in and out you will have to stay in.' With a boyfriend there?

Don't think so. Poor Alma. She was smart, though; she always found a way around things, like on a Friday night was my bath night and, because she was stuck in with me on bath night, she arranged for her mates to come round to ours. I hated it - a bath every week was bad enough - and only a half-closed kitchen door between. Some of them would then stay the night and I was the one with a big double bed. World War Two - the beginning of female dominance.

One night, I was playing out on the street with Peter Sparrow. We had just taken a bundle of newspapers to the fish and chip shop on Uxbridge Street, opposite Dale Street, in return for a couple of bags of batter bits, which was a deal most fish and chip shops would do during the war. We would then sit on the curb of the pavement and eat them. In fact, most people used to prefer eating fish and chips the traditional way, walking along the street with greasy fingers with salt and vinegar. We were wiping our sticky fingers which were now nice and clean having licked off all the grime and dirt from playing by eating and licking the grease from our batter bits.

I was looking at a small hole in the post office window; it was one large window and the hole was about 3ft from ground level. It looked like a pellet hole. The glass was flush on the outside with a hole but splayed on the inside, so the damage looked like a top of a mini volcano or a boil, so something had hit it from the outside, maybe a pellet or a stone flipped by a wheel. I noticed that the hole was in line with a shelf with birthday cards upon it, so I blew through this hole and managed to blow two of the cards down and this went on for ages. They kept putting the cards back up and I kept blowing them down. One evening I took a straw with me and it fitted into the hole well. They had two shelves with cards on and, because of the glass damage shape inside, I had a good radius. I managed to clear both shelves. I never tried again, but they never knew why their cards were down some mornings.

That hole was still there in that shop window when I moved from the area after the war.

Alma was in the Girl Guides now on the Branston Road somewhere. I had managed to join the Third Burton Cubs at the Christ Church hall, where we met early evening once a week. It was handy for me, a two-minute run from the house, and I wore my uniform: a green long-sleeved jumper; a round green cap with yellow braiding and badge; a green and yellow neckerchief with a leather woggle; a pair of green thick ribbon tabs that would hold up your long grey socks and be left on show under the turn of each sock below the knee on the outside of both legs; short grey trousers; sensible shoes and plain shirt. I liked being in the Cubs. We would learn about camping, ready for when we went up into the Scouts, how to pitch a tent and store rations. We would do some keep fit and always finish off learning a new knot, and practice ready for our test. I remember the master saying that we would not be shown firelighting until we were Scouts.

Mam quite liked me going to Cubs as she knew I wasn't running around the streets with my roughneck mates. I only got into the Cubs mainly because I was always hanging around outside and got to know them plus most of my gear was secondhand from the club. Mam used to make neckties and knit jumpers for them which would take care of my subs. I don't think that any of my street mates went to my school. Most went to Christ Church School or others and we were very mixed ages, just a bunch of kids that lived close to each other, boys and girls. The same hall was also used for Sunday school where I was made to attend as Mam was quite religious and Alma had taken Holy Communion - whatever that is. (First class ticket to heaven I think). Anyway, we used to sit in age groups around a preacher or helper, as they would read from the Bible mostly and I loved the stories of old and of Jesus and his disciples and the miracles. I am afraid the teacher, whose group I mostly got put into, was a lovely man, but he had this terrible stutter and I felt sorry and sad for him but showed my feelings by giggling whilst he was telling his story. The more I tried to stop the worse I got. When the lesson was over, we all said a prayer, sang a hymn and, as we filed out, I was getting dirty looks from many kids. It was okay for a few times and I ended up in different groups until it happened again.

One Sunday I was put back in his group. So, I thought it might be different this time - like at school – so this lovely man started to tell his story and his stutter was better than I remembered. I could feel the beads of sweat building up on my face; my eyes were starting to burn. He said, "And th-the m-m-man shouts l-l-lepers".

That was it. I just burst out laughing and that started another two kids off. So, I got put into a corner near the door facing the wall until the end of the lesson. I knew I was in trouble, but I still kept giggling when I thought of these leopards running around this blind man in the village square.

So as everyone was getting filed out, these girls were saying loudly, "Gordon Kent won't go to heaven when he dies". I then got told off and warned not to be so disruptive.

But it all happened again many weeks later and I was in the corner again, told off again, and I was genuinely sorry and did not know what to do.

What I started to do was get ready for Sunday school, walk in the direction of Christ Church, check back on Dale Street to make sure no one was watching me, check out Uxbridge Street then run across the road and keep running until I was hidden by the bend in the road and meet up with one of my mates. The trouble was I would be in my Sunday best and it was always difficult to keep clean when playing. I would normally meet up with Peter Sparrow and together we liked doing dare devil stuff and tree climbing.

I don't think anyone found out about me playing truant from Sunday school. I started going to a new Sunday school soon after, at the far end of Uxbridge Street just beyond my regular day school, where a few of my day school friends attended.

I was also able to call in on my Aunty Tess and see my elder cousins, Derek and Terry, en-route in Napier Street, which ran parallel with Uxbridge Street. They always seemed to be doing something interesting, like firing at some target with air rifles, proper bows and arrows, catapults, boxing, wrestling or swinging clubs like in the Navy. Derek would show me his Sea Cadet uniform.

It used to be a tough area in those days. I remember that my cousin Derek had a best mate called Cecil, who was also in the Sea Cadets, and they went on together to join the Royal Navy. They went to the Far East and all over the world, and to this day in their late eighties are still best friends and living in the same area. Derek, now 88, still runs the Burton Judo Club with his daughter Jane, who is a second Dan. Derek and I were to become close cousins with mutual respect for each other and have always loved doing things together and competing with each other. We both think that we have the edge on each other, but it is not important, and he should admit defeat. But at that moment back in time he was my hero. He was a bit older than Alma and a big influence on my young days of growing up, encouraging with his no-nonsense teachings. He will be mentioned frequently in my writing.

Sometimes Derek would put some hair cream on my hair and comb it to have a quiff at the front like his, so I would go on to Sunday school looking cool (so I thought). My hair was always a mess, it usually got combed once in the morning by Mam or Alma and that would be it until next morning. Sometimes Mam would put some liquid paraffin on it to try and keep it in order, but I used to complain as it used to run down my brow and the back of my ears when I started running about. I was always running about; I could not even walk up and down the stairs. Then Mam came home with a big jar of Brylcreem. It was the most famous hair cream and was always advertised on the billboards by Dennis Compton, who was our most famous cricketer of the time and was good looking with wavy black hair. I quite liked that and it smelt nice.

Alma said, 'You spoil him,' but it was mostly water that went on my head to hold my hair down for school and when that dried that was it until the next morning.

At my age it suited me. I didn't carry or want to carry a comb and the hair cream was for Sundays or occasions. I remember that big jar lasted forever. One thing I did always carry with me was a clean hanky every morning, and this became a lifetime habit.

I used to go straight home from Sunday school for Sunday dinner, as this was the only day we would sit down as a family to eat. Sunday dinner time was very important in those days, and most people would say grace before eating, usually by Mam even when Dad was there. On occasions, I would have to go from Sunday school to Grandma and Grandad's for dinner if there was to be a family meeting or get together, especially if any of the boys were on leave.

I did not like Sundays; in those days it was a proper day of rest and would be observed by all. If you tried to mow your front lawn (if you had one) you would probably get stoned. Even Tweedle-Dum seemed to get the message after his early morning call plus he was running out of hens. I was thinking his days were numbered.

I would have to stay in my Sunday best, not allowed to play if out or visiting: "don't run about", "sit up", "sit straight", "don't fidget", "be quiet". There were some really nice walks along the River Trent and flower gardens. We could hire row boats on the river and have picnics all along the river banks. There were lots of people taking walks, bumping into people they knew (or hoping to).

People would do lots of walking in those days and there wasn't much money about to do much else, hence the old chat up lines – may I walk with you- or – can I take you out. Great stuff when you are a hundred years old, but not when you are a young sprog.

There were no shops open, only the odd small shop that would be allowed to sell ice cream, lemonade and sweets if you had the coupons. I suppose all-in-all Sundays were a good idea where people could meet up, try to be nice to each other, get some exercise and put the world to rights. Except when Mam decided that we should go to church on Sunday evening as she often did. I so hated this.

We would mostly go to Christ Church just around the corner. I would be wearing my Sunday best, none of which would fit me properly as I was usually growing in or out of something, and I always seemed to have squeaky shoes. My tie always fitted and although I don't enjoy wearing a tie, I always did and still do as a show of respect.

Many years later when I was a teenager, and Grandma was staying at our new home for a spell, I was putting on my new grey trilby hat and straightening my tie in the living room mirror. She said, 'That's right, a man is not dressed unless he is wearing a hat and tie.'

I smiled back at her, gave her a kiss on the cheek, and went out the door to get the bus into town, knowing I was going to get some stick off my mates over my new hat. I did not mind that, all part of the game of pretending to be a man. My Grandma had a lot of sayings like that and I loved her.

Anyway, back to Sunday night: we would walk round to the Church. Mam would look very refined and Alma would look like her lady in waiting. I was dreading the whole thing as I knew what was coming. As soon as I entered a church, I felt guilty and the whole building was so daunting, especially when the organ started to play. The Vicar would always seem to be looking at me during his sermon and, although I loved music and singing, I could only sing about four notes and they were never in my key. So, we would be in the Church seated in a pew, the sermon would be over and now it was cringe time as we would all sing hymn number whatever. Now, there were not usually many people in the church. Ordinary people sang quietly unless there was a choir to spur on the congregation. But who needed a choir when we had got our Mam there? She had a great voice and perfect pitch; she knew it and was not shy to show it, much to my embarrassment. She could sing soft and gently or with power and, with the acoustics of a church, she sounded like a female version of Mario Lanza.

As I look back on these times, I can only say shame on me.

17

I seemed to be getting around more these days and was allowed a bit more freedom. I remember one early evening a bunch of us coming home from the canal where we had been fishing and mucking about. The canal was well past the far end of Dale Street and the dairy that was my boundary where we were.

It was getting dusk and we spotted my Mam and a couple more mothers of our gang coming towards us. They had been told by other kids that we had all gone down to the canal with fishing nets and jam jars early in the day and not been seen since. We all got told off for being out too late especially down at the canal, but we didn't get it too bad because our mams were pleased to see us all safe together and having fun. We didn't get wrapped in cotton wool in those days, plus the canal was always busy with barges, boats, people and the roads were safe and quiet, no mad rush. Only the trains went fast, so for us kids it was the end of a good summer's day.

It must have been the summer holiday, because we also used to go with our fishing nets and jam jars over to a place called the

Old Mill. It was quite a long walk but only one road to cross and that was the Branston Road, which led from Burton to Branston, Tamworth, Lichfield, and the South. My Auntie Flo lived on the Branston Road and her side gate was around the corner in the next street, which may have been called Old Mill Lane. This led down to The Old Mill land where we would have great fun. There was a big pond where we would catch tadpoles, sticklebacks, and tiny fish. We would take them home, watch the tadpoles turn into frogs and the sticklebacks turn upside down.

At first, I would go with Alma who often had one of her friends along and they would collect wild flowers and lavender and she would press some of the flowers into books and keep them for ever. When I was with Alma, we would usually call in on Aunty Flo for tea and biscuits. Alma always got on well with Aunty Flo, who was her Godmother. Aunty Flo was also Godmother to my cousin Derek, and I was told that they both lived with her at some stage early in their lives, whether at the same time or not I do not know.

Aunty Flo never had any children and separated or divorced her first husband around about this time. I can just remember him as a gentleman farmer type, with a chequered jacket and cap. He seemed okay, and if my sister spent time at Aunty Flo's in that house then it would explain how she knew all about the Old Mill.

On later occasions, when I went to the Mill taking any of my friends with me, I would call in on Aunty Flo provided that whoever was with me was presentable. She was a funny old biddy and well known for her grumpiness in and out of the family and there was always something wrong with her. She would always give us lemonade and biscuits and I grew to like her even though she always told me off for something. She was the eldest of Grandad and Grandma Skivington's children (three boys and three girls) and, in spite of her 'chronic' illnesses, went on to outlive them all. Like the old saying, "An old creaking gate will outlast a new one".

We were all into bows and arrows now after seeing Errol Flynn in the best ever *Robin Hood* film. We would go to the woods that ran alongside the edge of the Ox Hay, which had a stream running through it, where we would cut down branches to make our bows and arrows. We built a camp in the woods; it was great, and we would all talk about leaving home and living in the woods like our mate Robin and his merry men, and then we would get hungry and go home. We also had another camp nearer home on Meller's garden which was a piece of waste ground halfway down Dale Street. It had a brick air-raid shelter on it and a high brick wall right around it, except the open front from the roadside. On the left side facing was a row of houses with front doors on the roadside and an open access off the left garden wall to the courtyard. This led to the rear back doors and shared yard with outhouses. In the middle house lived our mate Brian Meller.

Brian Meller was a good swimmer and was always going down to the gravel pits just off the Branston Road with other kids for free swimming. My Mam did not want me to go there. Neither did I as I didn't like water. I never did go there but I was told how good Brian was at swimming and diving by the others.

One Saturday Brian, Peter Sparrow and I were in the Burton marketplace. At the end of the day the fruit and veg stall used to throw any fruit and veg they didn't want to take away into a big pile inside a brick-built compound in the corner of the market square. From there it would finally be sent off to pig farms, etc. but not until we kids had sorted out our fill. Sometimes we would get chased off, so we always tried to be orderly and not too noisy. Also, there would be old people picking out stuff, because most of it was good food or getting too ripe to keep in stock.

We kids loved it; we weren't too proud. My sister would have died of shame if she had ever seen me; as for Mam she was more of a realist but would not have liked me being spotted by people who knew our family.

Anyway, one time when we were in the market, we were giving a bit of lip to a couple of young chaps who were on a stall selling ladies' underwear. We told them about Brian's older sister who had just won a beauty contest and a film test, which was true. They gave him a pair of silk stockings to give to her and promised to give her some free items if she would pop down next week to see them. I heard that she was pleased with the stockings, but I don't know whether there was any follow up or film test. I wasn't into beauty queens then.

Brian was part of our gang for years, but I lost touch with him when I moved to a new area of Burton a few years later. He joined the army for National Service when he was eighteen and was in a guard's regiment. The last I heard of him he was splashed all over the national newspapers. Apparently, he was walking along Tower Bridge in London when he saw a man drowning in the River Thames, so he did no more than dive from the bridge into the water and save him as he would. (Top Dare-ee as we would say in our gang). We used to dare each other to do brave and mad things in the gang, so I know that he would not have hesitated to save a man's life plus being a good swimmer and diver. I don't know if he was on duty or not, but he did get a top medal from *The Queen* for his deed, one of the Crosses, I think.

Meller's garden was always a good meeting place for the street kids; no one bothered us there. We would sit on top of the high wall or mess around on the uneven waste ground. We would sit in our camp that had a tin roof - over which was thrown an old carpet to weigh it down and for camouflage. The place was a play area for us younger kids, which was great as we made up our own fun in those days and lived in our own pretend world which was far better than the real world.

The grown-ups seemed happy to leave us alone to do our own thing - at least we were safe-ish and close to home. I found these formative years of my childhood stood me in good stead throughout my life.

Though I did not seem to be learning much at school, I was learning about how to play and get along and stand up to other kids (and people). Mam had a new boyfriend now and I was not happy about this one; he seemed like a decent bloke, but he wasn't my Dad. I think his surname was Willday - a local chap and I think that Alma was seeing his younger brother or cousin as he had the same name. So I was outnumbered.

One day when Mam was going out with the boyfriend as he was opening the small gate for Mam, I could see she was in a good mood, so I said to her, 'Mam, can I use some of Dad's tools, I want to make a toy boat.'

She smiled at me and said, 'You had better ask (what's his name),' smiling at the boyfriend and not realising the put down it was to her knight in no armour. She said, 'He is in charge of that sort of thing now.'

He said to Mam: 'Well, what do you think?'

Mam said: 'Well, he chops up the firewood and I've seen him using tools anyway.'

So he said to me, 'Okay, but be careful and don't use anything sharp.'

By now I was dumbfounded as Mam said, 'Well, what do you say?'

I didn't normally have to be prompted to say please or thank you, but those were my Dad's tools and, although I had never used any from his box, I knew them all as I used to look at them a lot. I was still waiting for my

Dad to come home from the war and make something for me again.

This incident has stuck in my memory mainly because it infringes on one thing that we both shared: a lifelong love of quality hand tools and what they can achieve in the right hands.

So, I started to teach myself woodwork. I paid great respect to the tools as I did to the real owner. Dad had a couple of books in the shed of how to use tools and things to make and I also realised that although these books were more complicated than my school books, with drawings and measurements, I was taking in some of it and understood most of it. There was no one breathing over my shoulder and I had my own time to do it in. I was learning that on my own without any distractions or competition. I would get there in the end.

I was pretty much enjoying life at this time. Mam and Alma were doing their own things. I was fed well and looked after but a bit outnumbered in the home so was allowed plenty of freedom and playtime plus whilst Mam and Alma seemed contented with the situation, I didn't have to worry about looking after my Mam, getting married or leaving home.

Our gang was getting a bit wild now and used to venture further afield sometimes and, on a couple of occasions, got tangled up with other kids by going through their streets. Once we walked through a street on the way home from the Ox Hay where there was an ice factory and the street gang there confronted us. They were older than us and they said, "Who are you?"

Peter Sparrow said in his meanest terrifying voice, 'We are the Dale Street gang.'

These lads fell about laughing, so we ran and didn't stop until we got to New Street in the town, where we had to stop as we had Cecil's younger sister with us. That bunch of kids didn't even chase after us as we found out weeks later when we all became friends.

The school summer holiday of '44 was good fun. I really don't remember much of Mam's boyfriend, but family life was good, and I was into my own things with my scruffy mates.

Now it was time for school again. I think it was on our first day back. After the register had been called in the classroom we were marched back into the assembly and main hall, where they had set up a couple of tables and the kids who had school dinners were sent over to pay their dinner money near the stage, as was usual on a Monday morning.

Then we were told to join up with our class who were lining up to the tables where there were two nurses and a doctor. I think we were having a medical check-up and a needle or an inoculation in the top of an arm.

I went over to join my class and was put in place next to Christine who I shared a desk with. Anyhow, the headmistress told us all to take our tops off and hold onto them, so we did. Then I noticed the bigger lads in the other queue looking over at Christine who was standing in front of me and when she turned to speak to me, I could see why. She just smiled at me without a care in the world with her arms by her side making no attempt to hide or cover up. The old Captain spoke with the young girl student teacher who came over and gently asked Christine to put her vest back on which she did only to emphasise the points. She didn't mind any of it, she was always cool.

Back in class - same faces, same seats, same great teacher. I think I was doing a little bit better this term; I'd stopped worrying about my academic skills and was enjoying life more, plus I think that wise old teacher knew that I was listening and learning more when I was happy. I just wasn't very good at putting it down on paper in a literate way. Sometimes I would go to someone's house after my school dinner during the lunch break (dinner time we called it then) as a lot lived very close to the school. Boy or girl, they were all the same to me at that age. Mostly I liked to hang around the school after dinner playing games or doing a drawing for the Captain. So, this year was running quite smoothly for me.

My next stark memory was on the morning of November 27th 1944. I was off school sick, which was rare for me. I was getting better and was on my knees playing with our young dog, Betty, in the living room. Suddenly the whole house started shaking. The dog and I looked at each other and I remember my exact words to this day; I said: 'Don't worry, Betty, it's only an earthquake'. Ha-ha - even under pressure at that age I had a mad sense of humour.

Betty, a Manchester terrier, ran straight into her basket that was under the table and sat upright trembling and I sat under the table with her as we were told to do if there was an air raid. This was so different - everything kept shaking and I thought the house was about to collapse, but I didn't panic. This was my first experience of how I don't seem to lose it in a crisis, but it can catch up with me later. Mam had to go out for something so there was only Betty and me at home. I was concerned for Mam and knew it was not just our home because of the loud rumbling with it.

Then Mam came home, much to my relief. Apparently there had been a big explosion at an ammunition base on the edge of Burton, causing lots of damage in the town, leaving seventy dead or missing and a crater one hundred feet deep and two hundred and fifty yards wide, plus some local damage like school windows, chimneys and Christ Church steeple. The steeple was twisted and was leaning over so it had to be demolished, never to be rebuilt. The explosion was the loudest ever recorded in the world up until the Hiroshima A-bomb.

After the explosion, there was lots of repair work to do in and around Burton, but that was nothing new due to damage from raids. Most sites were just tidied up and left as a bombsite until after the war and I believe that the seventy people plus animals killed by the blast were all inside of the explosive core. I don't remember too much fuss going on about it at the time, but that is the way things were during the war because you never knew what was coming at you tomorrow.

Back at school things were fine, but I wish I'd had more confidence as I had so many questions and things that I would really like to understand. I was so far behind most of the others now I didn't dare put my hand up. I was always pretending to understand because I was terrified that the teacher would point to me for an answer or to complete his sentence or phrase to something that I was not taking in. The trouble was that I did not hate the subjects; I just could not keep up. I was still doing the blackboard drawings for the Captain for his history and geography lessons and he was still our class teacher, but we did go to other teachers for some subjects.

In the playground and outside of school with other kids of all ages, I had loads of confidence and always preferred older kids than myself to knock around with. I think that was because I was very physical and could hold my own, but inside a classroom I felt out of my depth and vulnerable. The weather was getting colder now, and I wasn't too bothered about staying home in the warm after tea.

I always had something going on at home. Mam had taught me how to do embroidery, which I really enjoyed doing. I could also knit simple things like a scarf or help to make patches and crochet for bed quilts. I would do lots of drawings, plus I had started painting with a cheap box of water paints. I enjoyed the learning process of any craft like having your paint too wet on cheap paper when trying to cover a large area. The paper goes all wavy and wobbly and dries that way, or you haven't mixed enough to cover a single area and can't get the same mix to complete. I also learnt how to shade in with a soft pencil without overlapping the bit I'd already done because I hadn't yet learned how to use my fingers for hatching.

I also had my comics now. Mam used to have the *Daily Mirror* delivered every day except on a Sunday when she would have the *News of the World*. She used to say she always had the *News of the World* on a Sunday because they always put a lovely nice large countrified picture on the front, which they did (yeah right). Anyhow, on the Saturday, Mam used to get Alma and me a couple of comics each. Mine were *Dandy* and *Beano*. I loved them; they were strip cartoons with bubble captions that I could understand, and I used to read them over and over. I loved the comic drawings and always used to think what a great way to earn a living, drawing funny pictures.

Alma had a more grown up comic with hardly any pictures. There was a young chap who lived down the end part of Dale Street who used to get American comics from the

American base and he would swap them four of ours for one American - unless it was *Superman*, then it was six of ours for one of Superman. Their comics were thicker and more colourful - our comics were only red and black print in those days.

18

It was around this time that Alma and I used to go off on excursions to different places. I remember one Saturday we went to Leicester for the day. I don't know how, but I think Mam gave Alma the money to get us out for the day.

We used to go to lots of places and, surprisingly, used to get on fine on these trips with just the two of us and out of our normal environment. I would be dressed in my "Sundays" and was well trained on how to behave and speak when required. As of now, no more embarrassing my Big Sister by insisting on chips instead of French fries in a restaurant. I think she could see that I was developing some independence, but we had some fun on these trips and I soon learned that she had a sense of humour and just how crafty she could be. I got sworn to secrecy on so many things.

We went into this massive shop in the middle of Leicester called "Lewis". I never knew a shop could be so big. We spent ages in there until we ended up at a cafeteria inside the store and we had tea (meal) there. We had collected tickets to see a live show at the theatre and were a bit early, so we decided to have a look at Pets Corner, also in the Lewis store.

We were laughing at some tiny white mice when Alma said, 'Shall we take a couple home with us - they are very cheap.'

I couldn't agree more, so we got the mice supplied in a little wooden box with a metal grid and air holes, straw and water, and that was put inside a carry bag. Then off we went to the theatre to see the show.

It was a variety show and top of the bill was a comedian called Derek Roy. I remember him well, mainly because his big St Bernard dog used to join him on the stage, but his jokes were too adult for me. He was very famous at the time and had his own radio show for years. I can't remember the supporting acts; I think that I was more worried about our pet mice escaping from underneath our seats; and to think that we still had to get out of the theatre, onto a train and all the way back to Burton and home (in the middle of a war). I said, 'We are like two spies with a special parcel.'

Alma said, 'Don't mention mice - we will empty the theatre.' (and train if we get that far I thought). And we did.

"Timothy White" and "Taylor", as they became known, arrived at their new home 2,

Dale Street, during the winter of 1944. I was very impressed by my big sister's daring. I was also impressed by the names she dreamed up for them, until a couple of years later when I noticed the same name above a chemist shop - ha, but it suited them. We got them a large cage with a wheel and toys. They were well fed, cleaned out regularly, kept on a shelf in the kitchen away from Mam's cats and they seemed fine.

Then one morning, Taylor was found dead in the cage, so he had a suitable burial in the back garden and Timmy lived on for a couple of years.

I remember other outings with my big sis. We, alone and away from home, always good. But in the home or around family always an atmosphere, even as adults.

We were now on the run up to Christmas 1944. I don't remember seeing very much of Mam's new boyfriend and maybe I don't want to remember. She would have been fairly discreet when I was around and knew that I would not have approved inwardly, but I never made any complaints or comments. I know he was never at any family gatherings, so it could all have been a flash in the pan, as the next thing I remember was Alma telling me not to mention Joe in front of Dad.

It must have been around this time that Dad had a short leave during or just after Christmas and Mam and Dad were made up again which was great. I remember his big heavy rifle leaning up against the inside of the front door and he brought me a German Meccano set from Holland. I can't remember much of that Christmas, except that we had a massive roast chicken on the table what used to be called Tweedle-Dum.

Alma kept saying things like, "Woo, you've got a whole leg to yourself" and "Isn't the meat lovely?"

I wasn't really too happy about eating my favourite sparring partner, but back then we didn't fuss about such things and it was all part of life. It was usual to buy hanging poultry from a butcher, take it home, gut it and pluck yourself to save money. All the kids would join in on plucking the feathers from a chicken whilst sneezing and laughing. Chicken was considered to be a luxury then and for most only to be had at Christmas time.

Butchers would drag a piece of carcass into the shop to chop and cut up on the wooden slab table to a customer's liking. Living next door to a cattle merchant and talking to the pigs over the door in the sty whilst Mam was cooking me a bacon butty, I would never relate one to the other in a sentimental way.

Although I missed Tweedle-Dum, it didn't stop me from running out in the street with his chopped off feet to play with. He had such big claws and when you pulled back on the sinews they would open and close.

Christmas was great fun as ever and, as I enjoyed my winter holidays, I was thinking what a lucky little brat I was and that next year looked even better.

-Tweedle Dum-
There was an old bird called Dum
Whose leg ended up in my tum
He used to stand proud and crow very loud
And I would tease him just for fun.
Then one day to my dismay
I was on the wrong side of his pen
And coming toward me as if he was chasing a hen.
So I started to flee but too slow for he
And I got pecked on the bum, the bum
And I got pecked on the bum.

W. Spokeshave

Some main events affecting the UK during the year of 1944:

January – start of Operation Steinbock (the "Baby Blitz") a nocturnal Luftwaffe bombing offensive targeting London area until May, but few aircraft reach the target area.

February 10th – PAYE (pay as you earn) tax system is introduced.

February 26th – last heavy air-raids on London.

March 10th – lifting of prohibition on married women working as teachers.

April 28th – Allied convoy T4, forming part of the amphibious Exercise Tiger (a full-scale rehearsal of the Normandy landings) in Start Bay, on the coastline of Devon, was attacked by E-boats, killing 750 American servicemen of the LSTs (Landing Ship, Tanks).

May – Bad weather and thunderstorms leading to severe flooding, particularly around Holmfirth, end of month.

June 5th – Final preparations for the Normandy landings take place in the south of England. Following a mild improvement in the weather over the English Channel to allow the following days landings to go ahead instead of today as planned, and the BBC sent a coded message to the underground resistance fighters in France warning that the invasion of Europe is about to be begin.

June 6th – D-Day for the Normandy landings - 155,000 Allied troops land on the beaches of Normandy in France, beginning Operation Overlord and the Invasion of Normandy.

June 13th – The first V1 flying bomb attack on London takes place. Eight civilians were killed in the blast. The bomb earns the nickname "doodlebug".

August 3rd – Education Act, promoted by Rab Butler, creates at Tripartite System of secondary education in England and Wales with Secondary Modern, Technical and Grammar schools, entrance being determined in most cases by the results of the Eleven Plus exam.

August 12th – The V1 flying bomb campaign against London by the Germans reaches its sixtieth day, with more than 6,000 deaths, 17,000 injuries and damage or destruction to around one million buildings.

August 20th – American Liberty ship SS Richard Montgomery is wrecked off the Nore sandbank in the Thames Estuary with around 1,400 tonnes of explosives on board, never recovered.

August 21st – Dumbarton Oaks Conference opens in Washington DC. Americans, British, Chinese, French, and Soviet representatives meet to plan the foundation of the United Nations.

September 7th – the Belgian government leaves the UK and returns to Belgium following the liberation of Brussels on the 3rd September.

September 8th – The V2 rocket attack on London takes place, striking in the Chiswick district of the city and resulting in the deaths of three people.

September 17th – restrictions imposed by the Blackout are relaxed.

September 25th – V2 rockets aimed at Ipswich and Norwich by the Germans miss their targets by a distance.

October 9th – Fourth Moscow Conference; Prime Minister Winston Churchill and Soviet Premier Joseph Stalin begin a nine-day conference in Moscow to discuss the future of Europe.

October 23rd – the Allies recognise the Charles de Gaulle cabinet as the provisional government of France.

November 12th – sinking of the German battleship Tirpitz by RAF Lancaster bombers.

November 22nd – Release of Laurence Olivier's *Henry V*, the first work of Shakespeare filmed in colour.

November 25th – A V2 rocket destroys the Woolworths store in New Cross Road, south-east London, killing 168, the highest death toll from one of these weapons. More than 100 people survive with injuries.

November 27th – RAF Fauld explosion. Between 3,450 and 3,930 tons (3,500 and 4,000 tonnes) of ordnance explodes at an underground storage depot in Staffordshire leaving about seventy-five dead, a reported damage radius of 1,300 metres (0.75 miles) and a crater depth of 100 metres (300 ft), one of the largest explosions in history and the largest on UK soil.

This was the 'earthquake' I described a few pages earlier

December 3rd – Home Guard is stood down.

December 19th – Council of Industrial Design established.

December 24th – Fifty German V1 flying bombs, air launched from Heinkel HE111 bombers flying over the North Sea, target Manchester, killing at least twenty-seven and injuring more than 100 in the Oldham area.

19

We are now into 1945 and, back at school, my class has moved into a different room and our new teacher is a lady. I don't sit with Christine any more. I am now seated on the left-hand side of the classroom as we have been segregated and I am seated with the rest of the dunces.

Our group were still on last year's books with big letters and pictures whilst the rest were on real books. It bothered me, but I tried not to worry too much about it, hoping that it would come to me like some other things did. I knew that I was okay at maths, but it took me longer than the others, as I could not show my working out for my correct answers, so I got accused of cheating. My methods of calculating were unorthodox and unacceptable when I had tried to show them and I hated being laughed at. (A lot of things I did were not the usual way and it took me many years to learn that it was okay).

Back then, I suppose when teaching thirty kids, with a war going on, they had to conform. So we all had some form of stress going on. A teacher would have to go along with the mainstream in order to achieve their required end of term standards. I think that our teachers were on the whole quite good and if you were not very bright, or a bit slow like me, then you would get left behind.

I don't think that the strict school discipline did us any harm either, especially with most of our dads being away at war. So I just had to put up with it and do my best and, without Christine helping me out, I was on my own for good or bad. I felt like a misfit because I knew that I wasn't stupid and did care about school. I knew that I wasn't clever like my big Sis. I tried to be tough at school, and I fooled most of the kids most of the time and, physically, I was. This became a lifetime habit. I did always enjoy school - the teachers, other kids, the dinners (yum) and playtime. I still enjoyed doing the blackboard drawings for the Captain for his new term, plus he continued to take our class for History and drama, including his wonderful stories.

Gordon Adams liked sitting next to me. I would look after him in the playground as he used to get bullied sometimes so I would stick up for him. He was a delicate lad with a good nature and I liked him. The other kids all knew by now how I loved a good rough and tumble. Anyway, he lived at a Doctor's surgery where his mam was the live-in caretaker and they had apartments in the building, which was near the Burton General Hospital. Anyhow, it was not too long before he showed me a couple of Punch and Judy hand puppets that he'd had for Christmas.

We called in my home after school and he always had to pass Dale Street on his way home anyway. Punch and Judy were the most famous puppets in the world then. They always made one think of fun and seaside.

When I realised we could both do silly voices, I came up with one of my first enterprising plans. By the time my Mam came home we were busy making a string of imitation sausages. As Gordon only had the two puppets we needed more props if we were going to put on a show. Mam dug out some material for us and even Alma got interested and offered to make us a policeman. Gordon's puppets were quite well made and were for a child's hands. This kept us happy and quiet for days on end.

My plan was to put a shelf across the door of Dad's shed with a heavy blanket hanging down to look like the front of a Punch and Judy stall. But it was better, because we had a large table behind us for our props and puppets to be on the ready. I drew and painted different backcloths that hung from two hooks of the shed roof beams, like a street, jailhouse, an avenue with trees, and we worked out a couple of scripts, practised with the puppets and props, and silly voices. (I remember how much I enjoyed the Goon show a few years later, as it so much reminded me of these days).

No one could see who was making all of these silly noises as we were crouched and hidden behind the doorway. This suited me and Gordon fine. In fact, I don't think either of us could have done it without the other one to bounce off or to blame. Whilst all this was going on over a time, Mam and Alma had decided to pull down the chicken pen and turn the area into a vegetable patch, during which Alma managed to put the garden fork through her big toe, and had to be cleaned up, stitched and bandaged up for a while, then was okay.

So now the big day had arrived and we were going to put on a show. We put the word about for 2pm the coming Saturday with 2d (two pence/tuppence) admission to include a beaker of lemonade and a piece of cake. We put boards on bricks across our narrow yard for seats and by 1:30 there was a queue of kids waiting outside the front big wooden gates.

Gordon and I were getting worried now, thinking what have we done; all of the hype and were we good enough?

Mam was good with this sort of thing and nothing but encouraging. We needn't have worried. They were laughing at the show so much that Gordon and I were ad-libbing bits in and over reacting the puppets and laughing so much at our own show and with relief.

It went down so well and, because there were more kids waiting outside the gates who could hear the laughter and wanted some, we did it all over again.

Mam had to bring out the dining chairs as well because there were some younger children with the second lot with their mothers who had to stay and, according to my Mam, they enjoyed it just by watching kids entertaining kids. We did it quite a few times after that, even for the school one free afternoon.

I was still going to Christ Church Cubs, my new Sunday school and seeing my cousins, Derek and Terry. I think Derek was going to join the Royal Navy; he was already in the cadets. I was thinking that I would like to be a cartoon artist when I grew up. I did so love my comics and the way the artists drew their characters to try and express their funny stories. Sometimes I copied them. I think I was good at copying, but I knew it was only for practice and you had to develop your own personality in whatever it is that you do, but second best was okay when you were young.

I seemed to be making a lot of new friends that year because I was allowed a bit more freedom and got around a bit more. Gordon Adams was a good little friend and even when I was off school sick, which was not very often, he would call in on his way home and bring my bottle of free milk from the school.

Peter Sparrow was still my best chum, but sometimes we didn't see each other for ages. I knew he had a lot of chores to do at home and had a hard time from his father who always seemed to be in a bad mood. Pete loved his mam and would do anything for her. I think the main reason why my Mam would include him in my spoils was when she had made some cakes and gave us a couple whilst they were hot.

He said, 'Can I take one for me mam please, Mrs Kent?'

That did it. She would often say to him after that, 'Here Peter, take this home for your mother,' handing him something that would be acceptable without insult, like half a cake.

My Mam was always cooking and baking, all the things that she learned whilst in service. During the war shortages and rationing no one would be ashamed to borrow a cup of sugar or the likes from a neighbour.

I had my own house chores to do after school before I was allowed out to play, such as, getting in the firewood and coal for the evening and morning and also for the kitchen boiler if required, wash or dry the dishes after tea, plus whatever came along according to the time of year or events.

Peter came out to play one day with his leg all grazed. He had literally got out of his bed on the wrong side, and gone straight through the floor and landed on an iron gas stove in the room below that was the communal kitchen below - that's how poor they were. I think there had been a fire from the kitchen below at some time that had damaged and weakened Peter's bedroom floor. There were not enough floorboards to cover the whole floor area and they had to be spread around a bit. It was an apartment house but I never went inside it and it used to smell like a poor house.

Cecil Taylor and his young sister also lived in this house and were in our gang. There was also a large family living in one of the end houses in Dale Street that smelt a bit. I remember waiting outside the open door of a corner house for a boy to finish his tea before coming out to play and that his Mam and Gran were sitting at each end of the table and all of the kids were standing up at the table eating, because they had no more chairs. The front door was wide open and I was the only one who felt embarrassed; it was normal for them and they were not ashamed (why should they be?).

Alma used to try and discourage me from playing with dirty scruffy kids, but I was one of them and I was one of their equals; it also made me realise what a lucky little boy I was to have such a resourceful and caring Mam.

I was eight years old now. I had a good birthday and a new pair of roller skates, which were all the rage. I loved and lived on them and soon became very confident and daring, doing stuff like jumping over things, rolling backwards, turning and stopping at speed by using a lamp post or head on into any solid object, using my hands and arms like train buffers. When I took them off to go in for my tea, I used to feel flat-footed as if I was glued to the floor and could not run or jump properly for a while, after wearing them for so long.

Roller skating became one of my favourite things to do, even on my own, as it gave me a sense of exhilarating freedom, and this stayed in me until I was considered too old to skate the streets. As I got older, especially if I was on holiday or at the seaside, I would always try to find a skating rink to go on, and even on ice skates which I also enjoyed. Instead of eight wheels all wanting to go in different directions, you only had two blades. Provided that one had really strong ankles, there was a good chance of standing up, until you tried to move your feet. That was when the blades as we (hem) called them, took over and slid your feet twice as far and twice as fast as you meant to, until you were holding the barrier handrail having almost reached the splits position. But it was all great fun and later in my story.

20

We are still in March 1945 and the mood of the people seems to be lifting.

Folks were saying things like "We have got the Huns on the run", although we still had some bombings killing people in the UK. They were mostly flying bombs and in isolated areas. It seemed that Hitler was too busy licking his wounds from his failed assault on Russia, and trying to hold out against the Russian Army from driving them out and continuing all the way into Germany.

The Americans, Brits and Allies were taking control of Europe ready for closure. Hitler's desert war was doomed, so little Britain would have to wait a while.

I used to listen to Mr Churchill when he made his many speeches in the evenings on the wireless. Mam used to let me stay up to listen to him and I did listen. Everyone had great respect for him and he had a wonderful way of speaking and I looked upon him like he was a member of our family, like an uncle. You could feel his emotions, his anger, calmness, cool determination and fearless courage of the British. I may not have understood a lot of what he was saying but it made me feel safer in my bed at night.

Around this time, Mam and I used to do a lot of things together and she would often take me to the pictures with her, which was great because sometimes it was an "A" film - that meant you had to have an adult with you to get in. One reason for Mam taking me around more was that Alma was now a teenager and wanted to be out with her mates more and doing their own thing, boys I suppose. I know I used to annoy her but it must have been a pain dragging me around and looking after me when I was younger.

Mam and me went to an exhibition around this time; I think it was held in the Jubilee Hall in town and it was a display of the ongoing war items, uniforms, weapons, etc. British and German. It was really good and we bought two cap badges. We kids collected all war trophies and did swaps.

I remember one film that Mam took me to see. It was called *Henry V* and it starred Laurence Olivier. Some of it was not easy for me to follow as it was written as a play by William Shakespeare, and they were trying to stay true to most of the dialog that was olde English. But in the main I really enjoyed it and so did Mam; she was raving about it afterwards. I knew about William Shakespeare from school and that he liked to throw flat stones to skim the top of the water of the river Avon as a boy, and about Ann Hathaway's cottage. I knew it was a story of the time based on some truth, and I loved the battle scenes with the medieval dress and armour all in colour. (Only big or epic films like this one would be in colour).

The only problem was I was booked in with the dentist next day to have a tooth out and I had a toothache and kept wondering throughout the film whether I was going to be okay at the dentist as I had never been to one before. I had only heard about all the mad stories we kids told each other about this big long needle that may go right through your jaw and the likes.

The funny thing is, as I write this story, I can't even remember my first visit to the dentist, only worrying about it.

Alma didn't want to go with us to see it as it was not her kind of film. She always seemed to be practical minded. It was the same with her music; she would practise her pieces and scales for a short while and that would be it. Then she would lock the lid and read a book.

I used to think, how can you have such a beautiful big instrument and not play with it more? I asked Mam if I could have lessons, but she couldn't afford it. My Grandad was going to teach me the violin like he was teaching Cousin Derek, so that was okay with me.

We were getting lots of positive news on the wireless regarding the war turning in our favour, like we were bombing Germany and infantry were moving along the borders in preparation for entry. The Russians were driving the Germans out of Russia all the way home and into Berlin. All good news - no more Lord Haw Haw, who used to cut in on our radio networks with propaganda speeches all through the war telling us to surrender, that Britain had no chance, and we were too weak against the might of the German Army. He was British but I am not sure that he was a real Lord.

Our factories were still working flat out to supply all the ammo and supplies needed for what we hoped would be the final push, but the British mood had lifted now that the war looked as if it was not only turning but that we were getting the upper hand. A lot of credit to our Allies - without whom it would not have been happening. Most of our supplies were also getting in and out of the country now that the German U-boats were losing their grip on the English Channel. The Spitfire in our skies had proved too much for the Luftwaffe.

Most people knew that the war went badly for us at first. Dunkirk was a terrible blow to our proud Nation. This was followed two weeks later by the sinking of the Lancastria on 17th June 1940, killing at least 4,000. It was the worst maritime disaster in British history, but kept quiet at the time so as not to demoralise the people too much with more bad news. This got swept under until all records became available seventy-five years later. Another thing that emerged from buried records was that during the evacuation of Dunkirk the RAF was nowhere to be seen, but records now prove that they were there all the time above the clouds fighting off the German planes and protecting our little boats and ships all the way to our shores. It seemed as though we never won any battles right up to El Alamein and then we never lost one after that victory.

It seemed like the only people with any idea what was going on in the war were the Brass Hats, who probably blackmailed the media into what news they should or shouldn't put out, otherwise their access to Home and War Office affairs would be baulked. (called freedom of speech). Understandable in many cases, especially during a war.

We used to think that our lads knew what was going on as they were in it, but in most cases they knew less than we did. They would be stuck out in some God forsaken place with no means of communication and waiting for orders from command on what to do next in their own little war, and realising what a luxury it was to have a bag of fish and chips with a pint of beer. So, when they came home on leave they would be reading up on all the old newspapers to catch up on their war – after first getting the results of their local football club and cricket scores.

Street life was good and I had joined the Saturday morning picture club that had recently started at the Electric picture house in town. It was great - only a few pence and it got packed out and noisy. Sometimes we had a good fight with other gangs outside in the alley or the graveyard at the back of the cinema. The films were good old 'uns, black and white and some silent movies but good, like Laurel and Hardy, Tom Mix, Keystone Cops and Harry Lloyd. The stunts in these old films were so daring they must have been on a death wish.

We would all get seated and whilst this was happening the theatre manager would be on the stage leading a sing-song that always included one that went, *We come along – on Saturday morning, greeting everybody with a smile – we come along on Saturday morning knowing it's well worth-while...* Then the show would start.

The usual format would be a couple of cartoons followed by some film that was being serialised, like *The Lone Ranger* or *Flash Gordon*, and then a main feature film, usually a B adventure or cowboy film. It was good and most mams were happy to pay because it gave their kids some fun in a safe place and got them out of the way on an important day for doing things.

The first time I went to the Saturday morning pictures was for free, because if you were a member and it was your birthday you got a birthday card and a free pass for yourself and a friend and were allowed to sit in the circle. And my big sis being on the committee, as she would be, set it up for me.

I think I took Gordon Adams with me on that day and we sat at the front of the circle so that we could see down into the stalls and pits as we used to call them. You could sit where you liked in the circle because only birthday or special guests were allowed up there so it was quiet.

I could see Alma down there along with about three other committee members trying to control and seat all the gremlins. She was wearing a white armband with black committee on it, and she was walking around with her left arm bent and holding her left hand limp like a dog with an injured paw, or she was about to play her piano.

So this was my turn to be embarrassed as I watched her doing her posh posy walk. Despite her airs and graces, woe betide any kid who didn't sit down if she told them to. She invented bouncing - bless.

News update

10th March – sixty-seven German prisoners of war tunnel their way out of Island Farm Camp 198 at Bridgend. It was the biggest escape attempt by German POWs in the UK during the War.

14th March – the RAF used the Grand Slam bomb for the first time on the Bielefeld railway viaduct.

27th March – last day of V2 rocket attacks aimed at the UK. One hits Hughes Mansions, Stepney in East London, killing 134 and the last falls in Orpington with one fatality.

29th March – the last V1 flying bomb attack on the UK took place. The last enemy action of any kind on British soil occurred when one struck Datchworth in Hertfordshire.

13th April – the first Scottish National Party Member of Parliament, Robert McIntyre, was elected to the Parliament of the United Kingdom after his victory at the Motherwell by-election.

15th April – British troops liberate the Bergen-Belsen concentration camp.

19th April – Geoffrey Fisher was new Archbishop of Canterbury. Sybil Campbell became the first female professional judge in the UK.

7th May – the SS Avondale Park was sunk at 11pm by German submarine U-2336 off the Firth of Forth with two killed. This was the last British-flagged merchant ship lost to German action.

At home we were all hoping for the war to end soon and knew that we were closing in on the Germans and Germany itself. It was all in the daily newspapers and newsreels at the pictures. There were even rumours that Hitler was dead.

21

On the 8th of May, it was broadcast that Adolf Hitler had indeed committed suicide eight days earlier and the collapse of the Nazi rule in Berlin. The Prime Minister Winston Churchill made a victory speech and appeared on the balcony of Buckingham Palace with King George VI, Queen Elizabeth and Princesses Elizabeth and Margaret.

On that day there were street parties all over the country. London was jam packed with people cheering from Hyde Park, Trafalgar Square, and all along the Mall up to the Palace. Back in Burton, I never saw people so happy; the streets had tables and seating along the middle of the roads, bunting and flags going from a bedroom window to a neighbour's window on the other side of the street, food and drinks on the tables - jelly, cakes, fruit, the lot. Everyone was shouting, singing, shaking hands, kissing and cuddling. Everybody seemed drunk with power and other stuff I suppose; after all we were in Burton−on−Trent, renowned all over the world for its beer.

And I never saw any fights. My gang even decided to go and visit other streets and crash their parties and I remember leading my lot playing an accordion that I had acquired from some adult. When we got to Paget Street, they had similar plans, so we all joined together. Half of them were in the Dale Street gang anyway, so we had a great afternoon going around the other nearby streets. We were picking up other kids along the way, and the grown-ups didn't mind as we were all safe and together, just noisy. Everyone was looking out for each other on that day.

At the end of that great day, people carried their belongings back into their homes. Dining chairs, settees and easy chairs had been brought out for the day and also occasional tables and their tea pots.

Mr Fraser was folding up some of the wooden tables that belonged to him and were stored under cover at the back of his shop on some lock-up open ground. I was helping Michael, his son, to clear the tops as I knew I would get some sweets for helping. Michael was sort of in our gang and not, as his parents did not like him mixing with us ruffs very much. A lot of the tables and stuff were from the Christ Church school and the hall. The big double wooden entrance gates that we shared with the Leedhams were opened up and a table set up in the entrance space for drinks, etc. and the brick entry was used as a cooler and storage. That was now closed as it was getting late and I was called in.

There were still a few stragglers, as always, drinking and chatting, but I was well used to that at No. 2 Dale Street after pub closing time. I didn't think that they would keep me awake that night. I was hoping to keep hold of that accordion, but the man came up to me, thanked me very much for taking care of it for him and off he went.

To my knowledge I never saw him again; perhaps he was German. So, I never became a famous accordion player, but it may have started me on my weight training as it was quite heavy to lug around for a couple of hours. It had a mind of its own and opened up too far until it was as tall as me before wrestling me to the ground, so it's just as well that it went back to its rightful owner. Although, I would have been better off not having the responsibility of it, looking back it was such a day I will never forget. Ask anyone who was there and they will tell you the same. And that accordion was a big part of my day.

The 8th of May 1945, known as VE Day, marked the end of WW2 in Europe. On the following day, 9th May, German forces in the

Channel Islands, the only occupied part of the British Isles, surrendered.

The war with Japan was still raging on, but that seemed like a different planet to us kids in Burton. We didn't know anything about the Far East, only what we saw on the newsreels at the pictures. We never even saw a black person until the Americans came to town and even the evacuees were looked upon as foreigners with their different accents. So, times were good for most of us.

We would all go into town at night to see the lights, as all the shops would be lit up and the lamp posts were back on. Everyone thought it was great, ha-ha. It was hardly Vegas, but I know which one I would rather do again. As the days passed by the shops were stocking more fruit, fresh food and all kinds of new items. The Army surplus store was for work boots and canvas packs, etc.

The grown-ups were writing and receiving lots of letters and sometimes the telegraph boy would cycle down the street and we would stop playing to see whose house he was going to with good or bad news.

Playing in the street started to get more difficult as time went by, as motor vehicles began to appear back on the roads.

Most things stayed on ration for quite a while after the war to allow for adjustments.

There were many to make, like women waiting for their men to come home, kids like Alma and me waiting for their Dads to come home, settling down as a family under very strange circumstances, all different but similar.

The little wife has now become a grown woman who can raise children under tremendous strain and hardship, work a machine in a factory sometimes on night shift, proving not only can she hold the fort, but she can also do what was considered a man's job. The women held things together during the war years and proved their equality and then some. The man of the house, back from a horrible war that he didn't start or deserve, now taking the responsibility for his family and needed a job of work whilst still carrying the traumas of war (no worries). We would all have to pick up the pieces and move on. For some it was harder than others, and for others it was not possible.

Like most, my Dad had decided to come out of the army after the War. So did my uncles, except for my uncle Bill (my Dad's brother) who decided to stay in. And why not? He had a very good war record and promotion. He had no other trade or skills because he was conscripted as soon as he was old enough and everything he knew about was Army taught. So, he made the Army his career and went on to have a very distinguished career, a happy marriage and raised my four great cousins.

Dad did not come home straight away and Mam said that we were going to a place called Barnard Castle to see him on a short visit before he came home for good. So, I told Michael Fraser that I was going to Barnard Castle to see my Dad in a few days' time, as we were playing together in the big back garden cum yard at the back of their shop. Ever since I helped with the clearing up after the street party, I was allowed to play with Michael in their back yard. It was great, as he had loads of toys and things to play on, but he was very spoilt and not allowed to play with the other kids. It didn't seem to bother him, but I liked him and we got on well.

As I was walking through the shop to go home, I always said "thank you and goodbye" to Mr and Mrs Fraser. They liked that because I had good manners as instilled into me by my Mam.

Michael said, 'Gordon says that he is going to a castle to see his Dad next week,' and Mr Fraser laughed and said, 'What castle? Is that Tutbury Castle, Newcastle?'

I said, 'No, Barnard Castle', to which Mr Fraser replied, 'There is no such place'. They all started laughing and, with that, I waved and left the shop. I think I was blushing and embarrassed as I was very sensitive and easily put down in those days. I kept wondering that if Mr Fraser, who was respected by all, said there is no such place as Barnard Castle, what did it mean?

I did tell Mam about the incident in Fraser's shop as I had a big mouth and I didn't want my Mam going around telling people that we were going to a place that didn't exist. When I told her, she just smiled and said, 'You can send them a postcard.'

I was happy and relieved with her reaction, as she could be over-protective sometimes and that was why I wouldn't tell her about some things at school. She knew that I was always getting into fights and trouble but that was kids' stuff and fine, and I don't think I even bothered sending a card anyway.

So, the day came for the three of us to go to Barnard Castle, a small market town in Yorkshire. It must have been during the summer because we were going to stay with a family of one of Dad's army mates for a few days. I know we also went to a town called Pontefract and that perhaps it was there that we stayed. Anyway, it was great; it was a mad family, loads of kids just like my street mates and we had loads of fun. Plus, my Dad and his mate were around, and Mam was happy.

Alma and I went for a walk around the area one day and we came across a small play area with swings, roundabout, and a slide, so we had a go on some of the things. Alma ended up on the top of the slide when two teenage boys came into the park and went directly to the slide. Alma was still sitting at the top; one boy went to the bottom of the slide and said to Alma, 'Come on down, I will catch you.'

Alma said, 'No, I'm scared,' and the other boy stood at the bottom of the steps.

I was really worried as I have never seen my sister scared before and, although I knew I would outrun them, I could not go and leave my sister to these boys. So, as they were talking, I was weighing up these two and didn't know what to do, as they were too big for me to take on, but there was no one about and I had no choice.

Alma knew me well enough to know that I would not run, so she said, 'Go and get Mum.'

The boys didn't look bothered with that, so I started to run toward the corner entrance gate when Alma shouted me to stop.

When I turned around she was down off the chute and talking to the boys. She shouted at me to stay where I was and she would join me. She stood chatting to the boys for a while and then they all walked a little way toward me, chatting away and parted waving hands at each other.

I never did work out how it all got resolved so quickly; I think she was just flirting with them. I would like to think that she wanted me clear out of reach before coming down the chute and eating those boys for breakfast, if it had been required. So, it all turned out well for three lucky boys - another "Don't tell Mam" episode.

I remember that it was great fun being wherever we were and staying with this mad family and seeing Dad. I think our Dads were barracked somewhere nearby because they weren't with us all of the time and were always in uniform. Anyway, on the last day Mam and her new friend went to the railway station to see off their hubbies who were being demobbed. We kids had to run down to the railway crossings where we sat on the fence. Dad and his mate waved to us as the train went by and it felt good. Alma said, 'Next time we see Dad he will be a civvy.'

Next day we said a hearty goodbye to our new friends and went home. I don't know if we ever saw them again, I think not – shame.

Back home, Mam and Alma had pulled down the chicken pen now that we didn't have chickens any more. They turned the run area into a vegetable patch with some flowers. Alma managed to put the garden fork through her big toe, but it healed up okay. I was glad to see the pen down 'cos it reminded me of my old sparring partner, Tweedle-Dum; I bet the neighbours didn't miss him.

Gordon Adams and I did a couple of our hand puppet shows knowing that it would be our last chance to use the shed doorway. With Dad coming home soon there would be no mates in the shed larking about, lying on top of the shed roof on dark nights eating the pig's roasted potatoes and rolling fags.

Oh no, time for some real discipline, but I wouldn't change a thing. I had a great family and was looking forward to my Dad coming home. It was a great summer.

The Ox Hay was full of fun and events through the summer holidays. There was a big marquee tent with shows on every day with all kinds of side shows and events spread around the field. It was packed every day with folks doing everything, joining in sports events, competitions, picnics, and boating as the river Trent flowed along the edge of the field. There were also lots of circus type performers. It was amazing how they had it all set up, considering that the only two ways onto the field were either walking down from the footbridge that led to the Ferry Bridge, or a small entrance gate leading from the Cherry Orchard on the other side of the field. The river was usually quite shallow in the summer, so they might have used that. The Ox Hay field would normally flood over once a year during the rainy season.

Although our war seemed to be over, there was still fierce fighting going on in the Far East against Japan. The Japanese were on their knees, but they would not surrender and were fighting on to their last man. To invade Japan itself would have resulted in horrific American and Allied casualties.

President Truman ordered that the new weapon, "Atomic Bomb", be dropped on Japan. This operation was carried out on August 6th 1945, when a five-ton bomb was dropped over the Japanese city of Hiroshima. This was not the planned target, but due to weather and other conditions it was decided upon as an alternative. This new bomb caused a massive loss of life, disruption and ongoing radiation effects.

After this first bomb, the Japanese still did not surrender, so it was decided that a second bomb would be dropped by the Americans. Three days later, on 9th August, the second 'A'

Bomb was dropped on the Japanese city of Nagasaki. This was followed by an immediate and unconditional surrender to the American Forces, who would probably give them a better deal than the Russians, who were also closing in on them. So, WW2 finally came to an end.

Summary of events 1945 – Cont. from VE Day:

9th May – German forces in the Channel Islands, the only occupied part of the British Isles, surrendered.

23rd May – Churchill formed a "caretaker" Conservative Party administration, pending an election, officially ending the wartime Coalition government.

28th May – William Joyce, known as "Lord Haw-Haw" was captured. He was charged with high treason in London for his English-language wartime broadcasts on German radio. He was hanged in January 1946.

1st June – the UK took over administration of Lebanon and Syria.

7th June – the Benjamin Britton opera, *Peter Grimes* first performed at the Sadler's Wells theatre in London.

13th June – Council for the Encouragement of Music and the Arts renamed Arts Council of Great Britain.

15th June – Parliament passed the Family Allowances Act to provide payments to families with children.

18th June – the demobilisation of the wartime armed forces begins.

Back in my little world the streets were still nice and quiet for playing in, as any additional cars and lorries were mainly used on the 'A' roads. Most of our deliveries were still done by horse and cart. Not much military stuff was available yet, so we were still whizzing around on our home-made four-wheeled trolleys and roller skates.

It was the summer holidays now and we tended to go further afield and liked to explore and find new places to play. If we saw any new kids in their area we would ask if we could play with them. That always seemed to work well at the end of the war - after all, we were British and stood together. The kids were picking up on the grown-ups' attitude and we made lots of new mates around the districts. It was good when you would bump into each other years later at clubs, scouts, night school and the like.

22

So, I am still in the summer of 1945.

It seemed to be a very busy year; everyone was full of optimism and prepared to work hard to get our country back on its feet. The war had been costly to all nations and, luckily, we had the Americans who assisted us in our recovery with trade and finance.

Meanwhile, back in the kids' summer holiday world, it was a great summer. We used to go down to the canal a lot. It was good there, and the canal was quite busy in those days with lots of barges going up and down to different towns all over the country. Some pulled by horse and most of them would be well painted and have a name, also a company name board on some. It was interesting and good fun and quite safe in the daylight. We would also go over to the Old Mill, on the other side of town and just off the Branston Road, near where my Aunty Flo lived.

As I have mentioned earlier, I would usually call in on Aunty Flo to say hello and use her toilet. This was an outside toilet with a large wooden seat; it was like a large low table about eighteen inches deep, eighteen inches high and went from wall to wall approx. three feet. The middle part was a hinged flap with a large hole in it under which a bucket would be placed (ha-hem). This would make it easy to lift in and out at slop out time when the waste would get buried in the back garden. This pine WC would be scrubbed once a week. Because Aunty Flo was very posh, she also had a lid that closed over the top of the hole and had a fly paper hanging up in a corner of the loo. I never knew whether Aunty Flo liked me or not, but she always gave us a lemonade and a biscuit or cake for me and anyone who was with me. She always moaned about everything and I knew that she thought I was spoilt.

All my cousins were scared of her. She never had any children of her own, but the one that she favoured was always my big sis, Alma. If I had not called in to say hello it would not have gone down very well if any of the family found out. It would have been considered rude and selfish to be over in the area and not call in (I agree) as most communications were word of mouth back then.

She did grow on me over the years when I got to know more about grown-ups. I would never call in on her on the way home because we would always be dirty with our jam jars full of tadpoles, sticklebacks and anything else that we had won on the day. Although the Old Mill was only a couple of miles from home, when you are just kids and haven't been anywhere or even on a train, a different area seems out of bounds and we would make a big deal of it when we got back to our street with our various assortments of creatures following our wildlife hunting expeditions. We would sort them out on the big slab at the bottom of our back garden to watch the tadpoles grow legs and turn into frogs.

Following our trip to Barnard Castle, my motley crew got into train spotting for a spell and we had a favourite place that we used to go to, not far from the end of Dale Street. There was a wide wall that we used to sit on to watch the trains go by and take down their numbers that used to be painted on the side of every steam engine, usually on both sides of the driver's door. Because we were not very far from the railway station, it meant that the trains would not be travelling too fast as they would be still picking up steam. This would make it easier to take its number. Sometimes a fast train that did not need to stop at the station would whizz by, blocking your view and you'd miss both numbers.

Trainspotting used to be quite a hobby then, even with grown-ups. Most of them would go onto a station platform which cost a penny, but us kids had a better use for a penny. I must admit we did place the odd coin onto the track to catch the next train to see if we could turn a ha'penny into a penny as they would end up much bigger after the train wheel had gone over them. They would be well mangled shapes and sizes if you could find them. There was a signal box in view from where we were between us and the station, so you had to be quick placing and retrieving your coin.

We looked out for each other and we had a long view. The nearest track was one way out of the station, but it was not clever, and we did not do it very often. I suppose it was one of our dares. You could buy pocket books for train spotting. They would contain all the train numbers, names, information, some pictures and a place to tick off when you saw a train. It seemed like a good hobby, but I soon got bored with it along with most other kids.

I can't remember exactly when my Dad came home, but I remember it well. It was about this time, the late summer of '45. It was so good having him home and I adored him. I used to watch him constantly when he made things; he seemed so apt. He got a job straight away as a long-distance lorry driver with the West Midland Road Services. He stayed with them until his retirement when they were then called British Road Services. He ended up as traffic controller in charge of eighty drivers at the Reading depot. But, back in '45, I remember turning the Cracker Law corner into Dale Street, coming home from play or school and seeing an army lorry parked outside of our house. As I got up to the big gate one of my playmates shouted, 'That's your Dad's lorry.' And it was. It was an ex-Army lorry, still in Army khaki with a canvas cover over a metal frame and it looked great. Dad used to call it his wagon; in fact, most drivers referred to their lorries as wagons whether they had covers or not. And so, we settled down into a proper family life, and these were my happiest days because I had it all.

My Dad started his new job doing deliveries all over the country. He would deliver stuff from Burton and usually bring back loads from another place on the return journey. There seemed to be so much industry in the Midlands. I remember that one of Dad's regular outgoing loads were roof and floor tiles from the Marley Tile factory at the sand pits of the Branston Road. They were one of the biggest tile supply companies in the country and Dad would deliver direct to the building sites. He was to take me with him sometimes. The shed was now pretty much out of bounds now and Dad soon sorted it out to the way he wanted. The first thing he made was a kitchen cabinet for Mam; it was a bit like a dresser; a two-door base cupboard made to fit inside a strong white enamelled tin top that had a lipped edge around the perimeter so that it sat over the wooden top of the base unit. I think it may have been the cover top of Mam's washing machine that never got used.

The washing machine was not powered, but it had an inbuilt metal dolly worked by turning a handle on the top hinged lid. The top of the new kitchen unit was made like a delft rack on top of a Welsh dresser. It had a top and bottom shelf and a pair of sliding doors in the middle, and the whole thing except the enamelled top was painted light green.

Everything in those days was painted green, brown or black, it seemed. That's one thing I liked about fairgrounds and some of the river barges was their gay bright colours. The only problem was that Dad did the same trick as Grandad Skivington did when he made that wheelbarrow inside his shed which was wider than the doorway. However, it was only the lip on the worktop, so he took some boards off the front side of the doorway and bowed the thin door frame with a piece of rope like a tourniquet to make it big enough to clear the unit worktop. Then he nailed the shed board back on and he fixed the top section on inside the kitchen.

Everyone said it was a good job, even Mrs Leedham's brother-in-law who was a carpenter. They did not have fitted kitchens then, even in the big houses; just a bigger prep area or centre wooden table. There would be units with cupboards, drawers, wall shelves for pots, pans, plates, with hooks under the bottom shelf for hanging utensils, cups, etc. Wooden chopping boards were all scrubbed after use as there were no laminates yet.

Dad was always up first in the mornings and, on a Sunday, he would usually cook the breakfast, the smell of which would soon get the rest of us on parade, as he always cooked a good Sunday breakfast. Then he would potter about in his shed and the small garden. I would get ready for Sunday school, Alma would do her piano practice, reading and school stuff, and Mam would be tidying the house: sorting out the washing for tomorrow, laying out clean clothing for Monday and preparing the dinner or picnic if it was a nice day and we were going out together for a walk. Walking and picnics were very fashionable in those days, especially just after the war and I did not mind the walks so much now Dad was around.

We would usually meet up with friends and relations with kids; that was fun. I liked to get off to Sunday school as soon as possible so that I could call in on my older cousins, Derek and Terry, and Mam would sometimes send things to give to Auntie Tess.

Uncle Tom was home from the war now and he would be getting ready to go across the road to the Napier Arms for the day. He was Mam's eldest brother and he was one of the "Desert Rats" in the Army. He used to rib me something rotten and loved to embarrass me and mimic me because I was polite to him. It would make Auntie Tess laugh as she would tell him to stop it.

He used to say to me, 'Oh it's little Lord Fauntleroy', and, 'how is the Queen Mother today?', referring to my Mam who was the only one who would stand up to him and give him a lecture.

He was a sod and I was too young to cope with him, but I liked him, and I think he'd had quite a war. Over the years we became mates especially when I became old enough to buy him a drink.

I think Derek was in the Navy Cadets and said that he was going to join the Royal Navy for six years. Once I remember him ironing his uniform and explaining to me that the reason why the bell bottom trousers were pleated horizontally across was to represent the seven seas.

After Sunday school, I would go straight home where Mam would have the table extension leaves out and the table would be set with china crockery and silver service, including serving bowls and spoons, onto one of her embroidered table cloths. We always had a good Sunday dinner, usually three courses. Mam and Dad were both good cooks and we all loved our food. Dad would usually have a small glass of beer on a Sunday with his dinner. He gave me a sip once and I swore that I would never touch the stuff as it made me shudder. Dad smiled.

We would always sit at the table after eating with percolated coffee, tea and pop. That's when Alma and I would get them talking about when they were both children living in the same village and we would all be full of laughter. Mam and Dad would enjoy telling their stories just as much as my sis and me enjoyed hearing them, over and over, just like the old Captain with his stories.

Then, after a while, Mam would say enough is enough and she would store away leftovers and suchlike. Alma and Mam would clear the table, wash, dry and put away large and valuable large items like serving bowls, lids, dinner plates, then Alma would wash up the rest and tidy up whilst I did the drying up.

Mam had already gone upstairs to join Dad for an afternoon sleep, after which Sis and I had to keep quiet. That suited Alma as she loved reading, but in the nice weather and, as I was older, I was allowed out so long as I didn't get dirty and was home for tea at 6pm.

If Alma or I had to leave the table for any reason like going around to a friend's, scouts, anything - we would have to say, 'Please may I leave the table?' Sunday or not - or to use the toilet, 'Please excuse me' was enough. Yet, despite Mam's strong religious beliefs we did not say grace before eating. We always did at school; maybe they didn't in the big posh houses where Mam seemed to get her impressions from.

It did not take Dad very long to find himself an allotment to rent, as he loved gardening, digging, weeding, and growing his own vegetables. I used to go with him on rare occasions, but he would give me mostly weeding jobs and I soon got bored. All I wanted to do was have a bonfire, eat the sandwiches and drink my pop.

Once I took one of my mates who actually enjoyed the gardening. Afterwards my Dad said to my Mam that the boy was a bad influence on me because he could not stop swearing all of the time. This was true; people did not swear very much back then and kids hardly ever, so he didn't come again.

I did not follow in Dad's footsteps for his love of gardening, but he loved it. I think he missed the countryside, the farm and living on a smallholding as a boy. I know he was okay with his own company, so his allotment gave him peace and solitude. It was about two miles from home off the Branston Road. He would often go there with his gardening wheelbarrow on a Sunday morning and get back with vegetables that he had grown, in time to be prepared and put in the pans for Sunday dinner. He used to love that. He would look around the table enjoying our greedy faces eating up all of his lovely fresh vegetables. Sometimes he would go to his allotment on his way home as his depot was nearby where he would park up most evenings.

He also had a small lock up shed on it and a deckchair. I get that bit.

23

We are still in the summer of '45 and Dad has a holiday due. So, we are all set to go to a place called Whitby to stay with the family of my Dad's army mate whose name I don't remember. Apparently, he and his mate could dig out a trench and be settled into it with all their kit before anyone else in the Army. I am really looking forward to this; it will be our first holiday together and I have never seen the sea.

We borrowed a couple of suitcases from the Leedham's next door as we were going by train, which would be another adventure for me. Dad didn't have a car until 1955. Ordinary people just did not have cars back then.

Anyway, I just loved the train and everything about it, such as when it roared into the station, whistles blowing, getting bigger and bigger and hissing to a halt so close to the platform that, as the conductor walked by with his flag and whistle and shouting, 'stand clear', he disappeared into the smoke that was billowing out of this beautiful monster. Then the doors were opened and it was all action as people were getting off the train with their baggage and wares; the guard's van at the end of the train was being loaded and unloaded by railway staff, and porters would assist the passengers on or off the train.

So, we were on the train in our own compartment in a carriage that had a corridor and a toilet. We were settled in and I could hear the doors being slammed shut by the guardsman walking by, checking as he walked to his van. This was followed by lots of flag waving and shouting. Then, the whistle blew and we were off. You could hear the buffers clapping together and feel the train shudder as it did a wheelie whilst getting a grip and gaining momentum.

Once we were out of Burton and into the country, moving at speed, I was listening to the wheels going along the track and it reminded me of when we went to Barnard Castle. This was when Mam said to Alma and me that the train was talking to us and saying (going to Dad – going to Dad – going to Dad – going to Dad). I started nodding my head in time to the rhythm and the beat caused by the wheels riding over the joins of the track. Mam and Alma knew pretty much how my mind worked and we all started simultaneously singing (going to Dad – going to Dad).

Dad looked on, confused, and when Mam explained he just smiled. He didn't show affection, but I think it pleased him. A little more into the journey Mam opened her bag and produced a flask, sandwiches and pop. What a great day - and it got better.

I don't remember if we had to change trains en route, but we finally arrived at Whitby: a small fishing town on the North Yorkshire Coast in England.

We were met at the station by our new friends and went direct to their home. It was a nice clean house, bigger than ours with two bay windows at the front which let in extra light.

I always remembered how nice and light it was there. We were very high up - as I was about to discover when my Mam said, after a short while when we had settled in, 'I think I will take the kids down to the sea before it gets dark, as it is already late afternoon, and Gordon has never seen the sea.'

With that, their young daughter, an only child, said that she wanted to go with us. The lady of the house said, 'Okay, we will all go together,' then 'I can show you the best way down, and we can bring fish and chips back with us for tea.'

So, we all shouted "yeah", not realising what a treat we were in for. The little girl was younger than me and I think her name was Christine, but I don't remember her surname or her parents' names at all.

So, off we all went down to the beach, as I thought to see the sea. I could not believe how steep and hard it was, even for a young fit kid like me - the locals must have had legs like tree trunks. Back then I remember the top of the hills were like (and may have been) railway sleepers laid across side by side with a tile batten nailed along at intervals to help grip with your feet. It must have been quite dangerous in the bad weather, but I loved it.

When we got down onto the jetty, it looked great just like in the movies. The sea looked magnificent and, as I rushed to look over the railings of the pier, I got my first surprise as there was no beach. All I could see was where the harbour wall butted up to the pier jetty, forming a corner of about three square yards of triangle-shaped sand, and even that was disappearing bit by bit.

I said to Mam, 'There is no beach,' and she said, 'Don't worry, it will be there tomorrow; the sea is coming in for high tide at the moment as it follows the moon.'

Then I remembered the old Captain telling us about it and seeing it on old movies, but I had never experienced it in real life.

It was now beginning to get dark, so we started to climb up to go for fish and chips and back to the house where the two men stayed to talk of old times in the war together.

As we started to climb the hill back, the lady of the house pointed to our left where there was the start of a pathway and steps, saying, 'Those are the famous 199 steps that lead up to the old abbey that you can just see at the top.'

You could see the old abbey ruins towering above everything and, in the dusk of the evening, it looked spooky in a majestic kind of way, with gravestones scattered everywhere that added to the atmosphere. She added that it inspired the story of *Dracula* and was used as a backdrop for the first Dracula movie in 1931 and *Count Dracula* in 1977. Many movies were made using Whitby as an ideal location for a good horror story.

When we got to the house with our fish and chips, we all decided that we would eat them out of the paper with our fingers - the proper way - and save washing up. And my next surprise - they were the nicest fish and chips I'd ever tasted. We were all happy - what a great day.

The next thing I remember is waking up to the seagulls. I couldn't believe the noise when I got up and asked what was wrong with the birds and why so many. I was told that the fishing boats were in and that the birds would follow them into the harbour for their share of the catch. I was loving every minute of this place; it was such an adventure - and I was even getting on with my sister.

After breakfast, we went down to the bay, where I was surprised to see so many fishing boats. The fishermen were washing and cleaning down their boats, sorting their nets, etc. The catch from their night's fishing had already gone to market except for a few packed in wooden boxes with ice waiting to be taken away. It all looked so busy in an organized way.

We looked on from the end pier. Some of the large nets were spread out on the beach to dry out, be checked for damage, repaired, untangled and rolled up ready for when they would be needed again. Some row boats were also on the beach for whatever reason. The beach looked quite big to me now, and the sea tide was still going out, but it did not look like I expected. I had only seen beaches on films and pictures, with golden sand and sand dunes with palm trees. Instead, it was brown sand with lots of stones running up to bigger stones, then boulders, rocks, caves and, as I was soon to learn, very slippery, but how I came to love it.

Dad bought himself a fishing line, hooks, and some bait from a little tackle shop on the corner opposite the pier in the bay. The line was much like a builder's line (it may have been). It was a dark brown cord wrapped around a small wooden frame that acted like a handle whilst and to twist it either way for more or less line when fishing.

So, I went with fisherman Dad onto the pier to try our luck, whist Mam and my sis went for a walk along the harbour. Dad and I walked about halfway along the pier and Dad set up on the right-hand side of the pier, as going out to sea, and threw his line over the railings and started to fish. As Dad was looking over the railing down into the sea, I started looking around and there were about six or seven people fishing on this pier at the time.

I was taking in the view and enjoying the sea air with the odd sea spray that were all new experiences for me. I could see the lighthouse further along and viewed more of the shoreline. Dad wasn't having much luck with his fishing and I don't think any of the others were either, although I did see a couple of small crabs getting thrown back in.

Then I noticed a man on the left side of the pier who had half a bucket full of fish; then he pulled up another one and that also went into his bucket. Then he rolled up his line, put that into his bucket and left. I looked around, saw that no one else had noticed, so I went over to Dad and told him what I had seen.

For once Dad was listening to me, so he pulled in his line and moved over to the other side of the pier, set himself up with his gear and empty bucket, except for a drop of water in anticipation of his catch. He put some bait on the hook and threw his line into the sea and almost straightaway he got a bite. This went on and on, until we heard Mam's voice shouting, 'Albert, be careful or you will end up in the sea.'

This was exactly what I was thinking a few catches ago as he struggled with each fish as it tried to slither away. Mam's timing was good as Dad was now going into overkill with his good run and already had plenty of biggish fish.

So, it was decided to go back to the house with our catch. I will always remember that day, in detail, on the pier with Dad like it was yesterday. He enjoyed it especially when he was leaving his fishing spot and other people were rushing to set up there. Ha-ha, that is exactly how we got it in the second place.

Mam also had a good day; she was chatting to the fishermen on the boats and managed to persuade the skipper on one of them to sell her a whole cod fish - as she would. She was to collect it early on Friday morning from his boat and it would cost her half a crown. She was to pretend that she was his cousin as they were not allowed to sell their catches in the harbour. She paid him there and then, 2/6 (two and six) nick-named half a dollar. Two shillings and sixpence could be in one silver coin called half a crown. It was our biggest coin, and worth thirty old pennies, or four pints of Burton Ale.

So, we were all happy with the day. The next thing that I recall is waking up to the gulls again after a good night's sleep. I did sleep very well in Whitby with the fresh sea air and the walking. I for one loved the sound of the seagulls in the morning, and also during the day; not that I needed any reminders of where I was, because the environment was so different from what I was used to.

After breakfast it was decided that some of us would go down to the beach as it was such a nice sunny day. I cannot remember who came down to the beach the first time, but I do know that Christine wanted to come along, and it was agreed that she could. I wasn't sure whether I liked the idea or not as she had already claimed me as her new boyfriend, and not only was she a girl, but much younger than me.

Alma took me upstairs to sort me out with my not much worn swimming trunks whilst the excited little girl was taken into one of the other bedrooms for the same purpose. As Alma was looking for our swimwear in the suitcase, Christine burst into our room shouting 'Gordon!'. She was jumping up and down, dancing, giggling and not wearing a stitch of clothing, not even shoes. Her mother came chasing in after her, apologised and led her out, still giggling.

I could feel myself going red in the face. Alma thought it was hilarious and was often to bring it up in conversation. I now agree it was funny and a great memory. She would not get away with it a few years later, but when you are an eight-year-old boy it is another one of those "dissolving" moments.

So, we were down on the beach now. We had a picnic with us and I was playing with my new found friend, Christine. We actually became good friends during my stay at Whitby, and it gave me a good excuse to play with a bucket and spade, building sandcastles and things. There were plenty of stones around and we were able to include them in our building. In fact, the beach was so interesting that I started collecting sea shells, coloured stones, and the like. I noticed some people were looking all over the beach, even in and around the rocks.

I said to the grown-ups, 'I think they have lost something.'

It was explained to me that they were beachcombing and probably hoping to find some Jet.

'What is Jet?' I enquired and was told, 'It's like a black stone, and jewellery and trinkets are made from it. There is a small place in the town where they work it. We will go to their shop before we leave.'

So, we were allowed to do some beachcombing as long as we kept in sight. The big stones and boulders at the ends of the beach were very slippery and mossy plus there always seemed to be lots of small crabs about. During my stay there, I found some interesting coloured stones and shells. I was interested in the way the sea had worn and shaped some of the stones. I did not find any Jet, but I did acquire a small unworked piece with a shiny side to it, as a sample, when we visited the shop later that week.

I am not sure how long we stayed at Whitby. I think it was ten days. Although it was not quite what I expected the seaside to be like, in many ways it was much more. I was soon to learn that there are many types of seaside places. There were no donkeys, deck chairs or Punch and Judy shows on the beach, but there were some real people repairing their boats and nets so that they could do what they loved, which was earning a living from the sea.

Following the aftermath of the war, Whitby never became a commercialised port, but remained a small fishing village community of friendly people. We did visit the little Jet shop in town as Mam had promised, and I was quite impressed by the way they carved it into items of jewellery. For many years I believed that it was from the wood washed up from the old jetties and thought that must be why they called it Jet. It did seem that the only way to acquire it was by beachcombing.

The origin of Whitby Jet dates back 182 billion years and was popular during the Roman Empire. It became popular again in the Victorian age, as Queen Victoria always wore black after the death of her beloved husband, Prince Albert. Apart from her crown, all her jewellery would be Whitby Jet.

Christine and I used to go winkle picking. We were shown what they were and the best way to remove them from the rocks. If we accidentally removed any snails or barnacles it would be okay to chuck them in the pan as well (I didn't think so; I wasn't even sure about the winkles yet). Back at the house we would chuck the winkles into a pan of boiling water for a while. Then we would take them out, one at a time to start, and find the round flat end shell that looked a bit like a sequin. We would pluck it off with a pin, stick the pin into the top of the winkle, curl it out of the shell (ha), dip it in some vinegar, pop it into our mouths, chew and continue until we got used to them. Good fun - when you are war kids you try anything.

One day we went along the coast in a small boat to a quaint old place called Robin Hood's Bay. I don't remember if we went ashore or not, but I do remember that it looked like a film set. I was hoping that we would keep close to the shore, as the massive expanse of water, when looking out to sea, was intimidating for me, bobbing up and down in this tiny boat. The choppy water was bouncing off the many rocks of the bay, and this instilled my high regard for the brave hands of hard-working fishermen who work the sea: they must be a special breed of men.

In town there was a good handicraft shop where I bought a small self-assembly kit of a model ship to keep me occupied on rainy days at Whitby. Alma and I were getting weekly pocket money now. I got to like model making and it became one of my hobbies, and so our first family holiday together drew to a close.

On the day of our return we were up and packed. Mam had already been down to the quay, picked up her fish that was all ready and waiting in a wooden box covered in ice, which she took to the railway station where she paid a small carriage fee to have it loaded onto the guard's van.

We said farewell to our friends and Whitby as we boarded the train and headed home to Burton, and I knew that Whitby would always be a special place to me. Although I was sad to leave it, I was happy to be going home.

I had missed my scruffy mates, and wanted to tell them all about my adventure. I missed Betty, our dog and old Beauty, all Mam's cats, my own room and the sense of freedom I found in and around the place I called home.

24

One of the first things to attend to on our arrival home was Mam's fish, so Dad carried the box down to the bottom of the garden and laid it down on top of the large stone slab. It looked like a small damp coffin. Dad got some cutters out of his shed to cut through the wires holding the box together. Mam had been advised not to open it until she was home as it was carefully wrapped in ice. Dad cut through the wires, lifted back the lid and pulled back a kind of wet gauze. Mam's face was a picture, as if to say "Didn't I do well?"

I didn't know a cod fish could be that big; it was massive. Mam said to Mrs Leedham over the fence, 'Come and look at this fish, Ivy. I will cut it up later and we can share it.'

The Leedhams had been keeping their eye on our pets and house whilst we were away. In fact, they owned our house.

Bubbles (Mam's favourite cat who wasn't really a cat but a superior being who spent a lot of his time in disguise as Mam's scarf or parrot) was already in his favourite position during the fish opening (Mam's shoulders) but showed little interest in the fish.

It surprised me and I mentioned it to Alma, who said that he would be when it was cooked and laid on a silver platter for him. We all laughed as he was more spoiled than the rest of us put together, but it was okay since we all loved Bubbles. He was a great cat, and in my whole life I have never seen a closer bond between a cat and a person.

So, I was allowed out of the way now for a while, so I changed my clothes and went to see who was about. I took out some sea shells to give away. As I was changing, there was a tap on the door and I heard Alma shout, 'He will be out in a minute, Peter.'

I was home.

My Dad had made me a scooter; he took the wheels off my old push trolley that was now broken and rotting away at the end of the garden, used some of the wood from it along with some other parts he had acquired and made me this scooter. They were becoming popular now just after the war, and we didn't play with our push trolleys much because that was kids' stuff, and the roads were getting busier with traffic.

My new scooter was great, like everything that Dad made. It would have been suitable for *Desperate Dan*. It had two good wheels that may have originated from my old push chair. They were proper metal spoked wheels, made like a bicycle wheel but with a solid white rubber tyre, and about six inches diameter. The rest was all solid wood, apart from his ingenious metalwork. This allowed the front upright and handlebars to pivot whilst keeping the strength at the lower point where the upright is fixed to the baseplate. At the back wheel he had made a small but more than adequate bracket. He had painted it Army Green, except for the handlebars and the footrest that were left in bare wood. I was chuffed with my new scooter; it was bigger than shop scooters and I was okay with that.

It was another piece of gym apparatus to me; it was big and heavy and went like the wind. It was easy to control, and it balanced well whether going slow or fast. I could ride it to a standstill like a bike and it made normal scooters look like *Meccano*. I thought that I had better not run into a car with it or I would dent the car; cars of the future would be a write-off.

The only problem was that my Dad was no painter. I think what he did was put two or three layers of green gloss top coat paint straight onto bare wood and then added more coats onto each layer without using any priming or undercoat paint. This meant that he would be painting on top of finishing paint with more of the same, and the new coats would pull on the previous as it would not be dry. I can remember coming home months later after play, with smudges of green paint on me, especially on a sunny day.

I don't think it ever did stop leaving its mark on me and my mates, because I always shared things with them, as we all did. I guess I was luckier than most.

Back at school, I told my old teacher, "the Captain" about my holiday at Whitby and showed him my small piece of Jet, which he knew all about. He asked me if I was aware of Captain Cook, the great explorer, who had strong ties with Whitby. I said "no".

He asked me if I was going back again and I said, 'yes, next year.'

He said, 'By then you will have learned about him in your history and geography lessons later this year and next year.'

I thought "good" as he would be the teacher who did those subjects, and I always seemed to get switched on in his lessons. My general school work was very poor, and I was in the bottom section for reading and our books had pictures and big letters. I was embarrassed and hated reading out loud, but I tried not to worry about it.

Sometimes we would copy from the blackboard and I used to copy the shape of the letters, like forgery, but I couldn't read the words. The teacher would say, 'That's better, but try and speed up.' We didn't take any of our books home or do any homework at that age.

Back home, things were great. I would usually go straight home from school; it was about a ten minute. run, unless I was calling in on a family member or a mate, or had a fight on.

We had lots of fights outside the school gates, and I quite liked a fight after school. I was not a bully but, because I was short, I used to get picked on. I would never back down to anyone, and I loved a rough and tumble. It was all great fun to me; I didn't mind the odd knock and we didn't carry knives and weapons to fight with. If you had a pen or pocket knife on you, which most of us did, it would not cross your mind to use it in a normal street fight - and kicking was looked on as cheating.

When I got home, I would quickly carry out any chores that I had to do, normally have a drink and a nibble of something like cake or tarts. Mam was always making cakes and pastries; then I was allowed out until tea time which could vary now that Dad was home.

The next thing Dad did was to make a general-purpose wheelbarrow. It was literally a large wooden box with a pair of wooden handles fixed to the sides at one end. It was fitted with a pair of old pram wheels that were fixed to the middle of the bottom underside by its original metal cross bar. It was strong and easy to push or pull and, because the wheels were in the middle, the handles would suit varying heights. The capacity would be about two or three tea chests full. Lots of households had a wooden wheelbarrow back then.

Dad needed it for taking stuff to and from his allotment and for plenty of household things, such as, shopping for heavy items. I ended up using it for all kinds of errands, like queuing up at the gasworks to buy a barrow full of coke, which helped spread the coal out during the winter months. Although I was a spoiled brat, I was now getting older and having to pull my weight in the running of our home.

I used to do most of the errands and collections with the barrow. I didn't mind and would often incorporate it with play. Betty, our little black terrier, would often come with me. She loved that old barrow and would stand inside it on her hind legs with her front paws resting on the front of the barrow with her head up. She would bark at any other dog she saw, as if she was riding in a chariot, showing off. Sometimes I used to run with her in the barrow and, if I went around a corner fast and shouting, she would slide to the corner of the barrow barking like mad.

She loved it, but she was not always so happy on the way back from some places. Then, she would either have to balance on top of things or lie down to balance. She would still enjoy it, even if she had to walk at the side of the barrow on her lead, which was rare. There were some places where I couldn't take her. The main problem with some of these errands was the waiting - always queues for everything.

One day I was running down the street towards Meller's garden: a piece of waste ground where we all used to meet up, when my friend, Peter, appeared from a side street and joined me for the couple of yards it took to reach there. I noticed that he was wearing new pumps and clean trousers. He was clean, and his hair was plastered down. He looked a bit sheepish and told me that he had just been to see his probation officer and would have to report once a week.

Apparently, he had got caught entering a shop at night and stealing a cake - of all things. He had sneaked into the bakers and cake shop on New Street and took, not just any old cake, but a display cake with icing from the front window. It was his mam's birthday, but he was copped. The irony was that the cake he stole was made of cardboard and plaster of Paris. He asked me not to tell the others, and I didn't, but when my Mam said that she had heard that Peter was on probation, and because he was always allowed in our home (a rare privilege even for me sometimes) I told her why.

That was it: 'Aww, I could have made him a cake for him to give his mam.'

I told her that we were away at the time in Whitby. Poor lad. Peter is now even more in her good books.

I don't think Pete minded the reputation of being on probation as much as the reason why. The gang never ribbed him about it anyhow; they all knew not to push him too far. It did affect him in the future as he would not want to do things too risky in case we got caught. He was never scared, but he knew that if he got caught again doing something that even looked unlawful they would put him away. He could not bear to leave his mam, and he knew they were keeping an eye on him as they were not happy with his home life.

25

We are now just into October 1945 and a massive Fair has arrived in town and was erected over the weekend. It is called Burton Statutes Fair and is held once a year on the first Monday and Tuesday of October. It has been running in some shape or form for many centuries.

I don't know why - I think it started as an annual trading meet, but I didn't care. I had never seen anything like it, not even in the movies. It went all the way down New Street, all the way around Market Place and Market Square and along the High Street up to the Electric Picture House. The opening times were 12 noon to 11pm Monday and 12 noon to 10pm Tuesday. I could hardly wait for it to open. I don't remember if I had school first or not, but I know that I was allowed to go to look around with Alma in the afternoon and have a go on a couple of things. I was given a couple of bob (shillings) because we were going to the fair after tea as a family.

My first impression was my amazement as to how so much stuff could be erected so quickly, and then how brightly coloured everything was with painted carved wood - just like some of the barges on the canal, but more so. There were flashing coloured light bulbs and the big noisy steam engine in the middle of the market place, blasting out organ music and supplying power to the dodgems, roundabouts, big wheel and so on. There were hot dogs, ice cream, first time ever candy floss, everyone laughing, shouting, screaming and squealing, all whilst waiting to go on the ghost train.

It was even better at night with Mam and Dad, and I remember getting told off for pushing my luck as I wanted to go on everything. We did not necessarily need money because there were lots of side shows for free - it was good fun. I managed to get an advance on my pocket money so that I could go again the next day with my mates, as long as I got home by 9pm.

I remember I saw my sister there with her friends and some boys. They gave me a shilling and Alma told me to be careful and don't be late home. In other words, "shoo". I bought a great bag of chips from New Street on the way home. The whole town seemed to turn out for the fair. It was really great; I think that it was included as part of the war ending celebrations and I was the right age to enjoy the whole thing.

Perhaps it was cancelled during the war, or had a low profile affair that I was too young for or unaware of, plus all the lights and bright colours would not have been allowed. But it was great and I would look forward to the next one, when Dad might win the prize he would have won if the man on the rifle stall had not realised that my Dad was a marksman and twisted his rifle site with some pliers. But he did get a badge. The trouble was my Dad was used to a couple of wheels on his gun, and a target you couldn't see.

By the end of next day, the fair had upped and left town, apparently to join up with others to form an even bigger "once a year" gathering called *The Nottingham Goose Fair*.

Back into my home routine, I was given a new task for the barrow; I was told to go and collect a barrow full of firewood from S.B.K. (Sharp Bros. & Knights). It was a very large joinery factory, on Shobnall Road, which was just over a mile from our house. On a Saturday morning they would sell an average size barrowful of wooden offcuts for sixpence, and you had to collect it between 0800 and 1200 hrs. You were only allowed one barrow load. Mam said that one a month should do her as it was starting wood she needed, i.e. kindling. I knew what she wanted, as I did the chopping for our firewood. We had a great hand chopper at home with a long curved blade, and it was always kept sharp.

So, off I went for my first time and I took Betty with me hoping that it would be okay. When I got near the main gates I could see a couple of barrows out the front, so I knew where to go. By the time I reached the gates they had been let in through a smaller gate in the railings and were starting to fill up their barrows from a big pile of wooden offcuts of all shapes and sizes. As I approached the man in a uniform, Betty was standing on her hind legs, wagging her tail and leaning towards him; she liked all uniforms.

The man said, 'What's his name?'

I said, 'Betty.'

He smiled and patted her; then said to me, 'Give us yer tanner,' that I was already handing out to him and added, 'Don't let her off the lead.'

I said, 'No sir,' and he let me through the small gate to help myself to the same pile that the other two were just leaving.

There was a good selection of wood, so I concentrated on blocks and boards that would chop up easily for fire starting. I was loaded up and came out using the main gate as there was a row of barrows now waiting their turn to go in. I waved to the guards on the gate and headed home with a little disgruntled person having to walk alongside with her lead looped around one of the barrow handles. When we got along the road to a quiet spot, I stopped and made a bit of a nest for her. I had put her blanket over one of the handles so that it didn't get buried under the wood and she was happy with that, but no running.

Although there was some weight there, it was dry joinery wood and an easy barrow to push. There were no hills, and I knew, even at that age, it was good for my muscles.

Once I had got it home, Mam was pleased and said, 'Just chop and select enough for a couple of days; then you can do the rest each day after school with your chores, and it will pack in the coalhouse more easily.'

It was not long before I hatched a new money-making plan of action. I knew that both of the shops in Dale Street sold firewood. It was chopped kindling, about 8 inches long, bound together as a bundle in a wire tourniquet about 6 inches diameter and sold for 2d a bundle. When I saw how much area was taken up after cutting and chopping the wood, one barrow load would now be three or more.

So I said to Peter, 'Why don't I go to SBK. on Saturday, buy a load of wood using some of my pocket money, bring it home to our yard and start chopping it up?'

He could join me after he finished his Saturday job.

Peter had a Saturday job, 9 till 12, working for a shoe shop in town. I remember he did their deliveries on this big old heavy bicycle that had a big square metal framed carrier at the front, a flat carrier behind the seat over the back wheel and a large black metal advertising sheet fitted underneath the crossbar with the name of the shop on it. I think it was Howards – you would not win any races on it.

Anyway, Peter was up for it and he always gave all his shop money to his Mam. After I took out my tanner we would share the rest of whatever.

The first Saturday came, and I went and got the wood. I left home early, as I knew the factory siren went off at 7:30 a.m. for the workers. Just about everyone worked on Saturday mornings then. Betty always came. As arranged, I tipped all the wood out of the barrow and started to refill it with kindling. As I made it, Peter joined me and started mucking in whilst I was called in for a proper breakfast. It was also Mam's excuse to give Peter a cuppa and bacon butty.

After this we decided to try our luck with our first load, so we put two buckets on the barrow handles, told Betty to "stay" and went out through the big gates of our entrance.

Mam smiled and said, 'I wonder which one of you will be tapping on the doors.' That was the trouble with my Mam, always outspoken.

So, Peter went into action while I took charge of the transport and loading. The two buckets on the handles were loaded beforehand, but we decided to start down the bottom of Paget Street, away from the shops and our own street, just to try our luck at first. We agreed to sell them at 2d a bucket knowing that they would be getting twice as much than the shops. So, off Pete went to do his thing.

We need not have been worried; folks were asking for two and even three buckets, and saying, 'Don't forget us next time.' By the time we got back onto Dale Street we had two empty buckets in an empty barrow. A couple of people who knew what we were up to said, 'Don't forget us,' so we just carried on until we had sold every stick.

We then went back to my place, put away the barrow and buckets and swept the yard down. We sat on the yard pathway. Peter took the money from his pocket and scattered it on the brick paving. He gave me my 6d stake money and we shared the rest whilst eating cake and supping tea that I was beginning to like the taste of.

Mam said, 'I expect you're both going to the pictures now.'

We both said, "Yes", as that was our plan if we'd made enough money. We had, so we could do the afternoon matinee and a bag of chips on the way home.

This became a regular thing for Peter and me on most Saturdays. Once we got into the swing, and with regular customers, it did not take us very long. I preferred it to the Saturday morning pictures.

We are rolling into November 1945 now. Our firewood venture is doing a roaring trade - not that there is any profit left by the end of Saturday nights, but it's a fun day, and we now have a bigger fire to prepare for. We have started dragging anything that burns along to Meller's garden where we have started to build a bonfire for November 5th.

Some girls are making a guy, and the plan is to take it on the streets asking passers-by – a penny for the guy – but I am ordered, not allowed, on that one. Some folks are giving us old furniture now that the war is over and people are slowly getting new things and trying to do their homes up.

A lot of the grown-ups were showing interest and, one chap, who was one of our air raid wardens during the war and was a local, volunteered to keep his eye on it as it grew, in case some bright spark decided to throw a match on it one dark night. He would oversee the proceedings and controlling of the fireworks, much to everyone's approval. We were told to form a separate pile, as we had accumulated so much, and that we would pile it up and secure the guy on the top just before lighting time on the 5th. The rest could then go on through the night.

The local people were taking the advantage to get rid of burnable rubbish as, after the war, no open fires were allowed. The guy looked good sat in his push chair; he even had a demob trilby hat on, and an embroidered smile on his likewise face, and tache, so must have known he was in for a warm send off. So, he did his little tour and collected quite a few pennies which, of course, went on fireworks.

Nearly every shop sold fireworks for bonfire night. There were no strict Health and Safety laws then, even though it was only just the end of all the bombings. Then again, after such a war, a few bonfires and fireworks would have seemed small fry and fun.

Anyway, our guy ended up sitting in an armchair on top of his fire, and it was a great night. Lots of people with their small children, plenty of fireworks, roast potatoes and no accidents that I knew of. I stayed till quite late when it got very cold and I went home to bed and slept like a log. In the morning I woke up with sore eyes and a sore throat, but it soon cleared. I so enjoyed my first memorable 5th of November and the build-up to it, and it was something else to look forward to for next year.

26

Things rolled along quite nicely over the next few weeks. The weather was cold, and I was happy to stay indoors more. After school I would play in the street up until 6:45pm then run in to listen to *Dick Barton, Special Agent* on the wireless every evening on weekdays, for half an hour. It was very popular and the weekly episodes would be repeated in one run on the Saturday morning.

I liked listening to the wireless whilst doing things, like drawing, painting, embroidery, etc. I liked all music, fun shows, *The Caroll Levis Discovery Show* (a talent show), *Paul Temple*, (detective), and a man named Valentyle Dyall. He used to tell ghost stories and was nick-named "The Man in Black". He was on late and I was not always allowed to stay up for that. I am sure the only reason I was allowed to stay up to listen to him was that Mam and Alma loved to watch my face and the way I used to fly up the stairs to jump under the covers after his stories. He had a very deep voice and would speak slowly – ha - I think my whole family were sadists including me.

I was still rubbish at school, the firewood was still on, and I was trying to save a shilling each week so that I could buy some Christmas presents for the whole family.

My cousin Terry and I had decided that we would go to town together as he was trying to save for the same. We were allowed to pal around again as long as we didn't play hangman's tree any more. He was a couple of years older than me, but we got on well, always did.

Mam wanted to put on a big family party this Christmas now that all of my uncles were home from the war and new wives, girlfriends and children were coming along. My Mam became quite famed for her parties; she was so good at it.

Continued brief summary of events this year:
15th June – Parliament passes the Family Allowances Act to provide payments to families with children.

18th June – the demobilisation of the wartime armed forces begins.

26th July – general election results are announced, Winston Churchill resigns as prime minister after his Conservative Party is soundly defeated by the Labour Party who have a majority of 146 seats, and Clement Attlee becomes the new prime minister.

29th July – the BBC Light Programme radio station is launched, aimed at mainstream light entertainment and music.

14th Aug – Polish and Jewish orphans, liberated from Theresienstadt concentration camp arrive in England for rehabilitation.

15th Aug – VJ Day is celebrated in the UK following the Japanese surrender.

30th Aug – British sovereignty of Hong Kong is restored following the end of the Japanese occupation of the territory.

2nd Sept – Press Censorship ends. Lend-lease from the United States terminates.

2nd Oct – Piccadilly Circus tube station becomes the first to be lit by fluorescent light.

24th Oct – the British government signs the United Nations Charter.

15th Nov – Gainsborough Pictures releases the period melodrama *The Wicked Lady* starring Margaret Lockwood, Patricia Roc and James Mason.

26th Nov – J. Arthur Rank releases David Lean's film of Noel Coward's *Brief Encounter* staring Celia Johnson and Trevor Howard.

28th Nov – British fascist John Amery pleads guilty to treason and is immediately sentenced to hang.

December – Alexander Fleming and Ernst Boris Chain win the Nobel Prize in physiology of Medicine jointly with Howard Florey for the discovery of penicillin and its curative effect in various infectious diseases.

December – John Maynard Keynes secures a fifty-year $3,750,000,000 Anglo-American loan for the Government from the United States at 2%, effective from 1946.

10th Dec – forced repatriation of Liverpool Chinese seamen begins.

10th Dec – Bernard Lovell established the Jodrell Bank Observatory in Cheshire.

31st Dec – Britain receives its first shipment of bananas since the beginning of the war.

No date – The grammar school at Windermere reorganises itself to become Britain's first comprehensive school.

27

The run up to Christmas 1945 was good. All of the shops were going flat out to show the Christmas spirit with lights and decorations, lots of new items, and things we had never seen before, like window dressing, food and fruit, bananas everywhere now, and toys.

People used to go into town to look at the shops, with no money; then come away and try to save up for something they had seen. Shoplifting was a thing of the future.

My cousin Terry and I went Christmas shopping together, as we had planned, with our individual monies that we had saved. This was the first time we had done this, and I remember that we went two Saturdays on the trot, partly because we both needed more money to complete our lists, and because we took care and time having a good look around choosing what to buy for whom and the cost.

We both had our individual budgets and did not want to buy the same auntie the same brooch each.

I enjoyed those shopping days with Terry; he was the tearaway scoundrel of the family, but I was impressed with his patience, care and fairness when spending his own money on Christmas gifts for his cousins, aunts and uncles.

We decided that we would not buy each other a present as we were both stretched to buy all the gifts that we wanted to. Most of our Christmas shopping came from Woolworths, always the most popular store at Christmas, for obvious reasons. Terry and I did this for the next couple of years. We would take the presents home, wrap them up with name cards on each, and we would give them out together at my Mam's big party that she did every Christmas.

Most of mine and Alma's Christmas presents came direct from Santa Claus in a full pillow case which was placed on the end of our beds whilst we slept. I have known about Father Christmas for quite a while now, but one has to go along with things for the sake of the parents who love it all so much. You don't grow up in the streets during a war without having to grow up a bit quick in some ways.

So, it was about 6am Christmas morning 1945 and I could feel the pillow case at the bottom of the bed with my feet through the bed sheets. I knew what it was because I overheard Santa ask my Mam where he should place it earlier: 'On the end of the bed,' she whispered back (bless).

I went back to sleep. When I finally awoke it was still dark, but I knew there was little chance of going back to sleep again. I didn't have a clock in my room, (what would be the point as I still could not read the time properly?) It was very cold and I was quite happy to just lie in my bed and savour the moment.

After a short while, Alma came into my room, put the light on and jumped into my bed. She was carrying one of her presents, still in its wrapping. She said, 'The deal was that if we woke up before Mam and Dad, that we could open one of our presents until we were both called into their bedroom.'

'Have you opened anything yet?'

I said, 'No,' so I reached over and took the top parcel from my pillowcase.

She said, 'You first.'

I guessed by the shape that it was a book, so I carefully took the wrapper off to reveal this beautiful hardcover book called *Black Beauty*.

Alma knew my problem and said that Dad would like to see me reading some real books and not comics all the time. She showed me some of the really good picture drawings inside to help the story along, saying that it was a great story all about a horse.

I understood and was not ungrateful, but a bit out of my depth for now, but this book did end up being the first reading book that I read cover to cover, but not for a while yet.

Alma opened her present and it was equally boring. It was a brand-new brown leather satchel for school, but she was delighted.

Then we got called into Mam and Dad's room with our presents. I jumped into the bed next to Dad, whilst Alma sat on the bed round Mam's side, and so began just about the best Christmas I ever had.

I had some good presents that year. I didn't have a big special present, but a good variety of really useful things like model kits to make, and a hobbies tool kit with a new fretsaw. I was told that I could use the small wooden table in the kitchen to work on, as long as I always cleaned up afterwards, and that I could keep my kit on the bottom wall shelf of the scullery. I got paints, drawing books and paper, as I always needed those things. I did get a couple more books as well as *Black Beauty*, but they were annuals which I liked, loads of pictures and easy reading, so I was very happy as it was a cold winter. After all, who would want a new pair of roller skates on a cold wet and windy Christmas morning? - I already had that T-shirt.

Alma and I stacked our own presents into our rooms; then we mucked in together, folding up the wrapping paper for reuse, clearing up any mess and making the beds, whilst Mam and Dad went downstairs to cook the breakfast and prepare the dinner. Then we got called down for breakfast cooked by Dad - a fry up.

Yes, one must always eat a large fried breakfast a few hours before tackling a big Christmas dinner. Mam always used to say that Dad was a better cook than her, but I am not sure about that one - Dad never underdid anything. Whether digging a garden, working in wood, driving his lorry - "thorough" was his motto.

I loved his cooking, especially when you tried to cut his bacon with your knife and fork and the bacon flew off your plate in different directions, because you did not lay a wet tomato over it first. But I loved it: pork scratchings for breakfast.

I also remember, with a smile, how he used to eat a fried egg. I would watch him from the corner of my eye as he would carefully keep cutting off the white of his egg as he ate the rest of his breakfast, until he ended up with nothing else on his plate except the intact egg yolk. He would then carefully slide his fork underneath the egg and eat it like an oyster. I never mentioned this to him, but always wondered why he did it. Personally, I like to puncture my egg straight off and spread it over as much as possible. But it was great to have Dad home and to sit at the table together, just our own little family.

There were still some presents under the Christmas tree, but they were not to be opened until Mam's party tomorrow, as there were other presents there for and from cousins, aunties and uncles.

After breakfast, I got washed and dressed and was encouraged to go out and play until dinner time, but I had to wear my Sunday clothes and would have been ordered to play nicely - whatever that meant.

I knew the house was going to be busy with a big chicken already in the oven and all the frills. Mam and Alma were in and out of the kitchen.

Poor Dad. I know where I would have been going if I were him, but Dad and his brother Bill were never big drinkers, unlike the Skivington side of our family. He would have been busy on something, as he never did anything that he did not want to do.

Outside, I would meet up with the gang and we would decide what to do, depending on the weather, money and time. Even money was not much good today as there was nowhere open except the pubs until dinner time, and we did not want to sit in a pub back yard or the off-licence with a bottle of pop and a packet of crisps in between a big breakfast and a massive Christmas dinner, even though it was one of our little treats when we pooled our money. We would always get too noisy and be moved on when the landlord realised that we had no money left - ha - just like being a grown-up, really.

Some of us would be wearing new clothes, such as a jumper or shoes or socks or short pants. I loved wearing short trousers and would not wear long trousers until I was fifteen, and I honestly never felt cold legs.

We just mucked about, chatting with each other, playing snobs, which we would make out of lead. We would also play marbles, fag cards, hopscotch and many other games. If it rained, we would play in the entrance, and we were never stumped for a laugh.

Then we started getting called in, so we all went home for dinner. As soon as I climbed through the wicket door of the main door gates, instead of the usual smell of hay and petrol, all I could smell was roast chicken. I just followed the smell through the entry like one of the kids in the *Bisto* adverts. When I got to the big yard, both the Leedhams' and our kitchen doors were open, so I was copping both whiffing at me – then I knew that I was ready for my dinner. This Christmas dinner will stay in my mind forever. Perfection is the word; not only the cooking, but the presentation.

As soon as I entered the kitchen I was told to wash my hands, and when I walked through the door to sit at the table I could not believe this was all for four people. Mam's best china dinner set was set out for silver service, with polished silver cutlery including serving spoons. There were matching vegetable bowls, dishes with lids that allowed the ladle or spoon to remain inside the bowl when replaced, to keep hot, plus lots of smaller matching items I had never seen before, all placed on a beautiful embroidered table cloth with matching napkins that I remember her making during the war. Plus a Christmas cracker placed above one's Christmas pudding spoon.

So, we all sat at our places. Dad carved the chicken. We men had a leg each and the ladies preferred breast. Alma thought eating a chicken leg in your hands was uncouth.

Mam said, 'Put your own veg on, but don't start eating yet,' so we did.

Mam helped me with mine because I didn't understand half of what was on the table. So, when we were ready we just sat there, and Mam clasped her hands together and started to pray; so we also clasped our hands, even Dad. She said a short prayer and as she said 'amen' started to cry. So did me and sis. Dad didn't, not quite; it was about him coming home to us.

Then we were ordered to pull our crackers, put on our silly hats that were inside, shout *Merry Christmas* and tuck in. I had to tuck my hat into the top of my glasses as it kept falling over my face and covering my mouth. I only had a small head then, but a big mouth. I had to save some of the leg for my supper because I needed more room for Mam's lovely home-made Christmas pudding.

Alma could not help asking me whilst eating my chicken leg in my hands just like my Dad was, if it tasted as nice as Dum-Dums'. She couldn't help being nasty, but was improving as I got older.

After Christmas dinner, Dad and I went into the front room where there was a nice open fire. Dad was asleep in no time and I played with small Christmas toys and books.

I would not go out any more that day as it was quite cold and would be dark soon, and it was so cosy inside our little home.

Mam and Alma were clearing up the after-dinner stuff and laying out the table for tomorrow's whole family party. It was ridiculous; all of the food in the pantry and kitchen, ready and waiting to be laid out on the table tomorrow as an ongoing "help yourself" buffet. They had been cooking for days: mince pies, tarts, small cakes, big cakes, trifles, jellies – the lot. I was told not to slam the back door when running in and out whilst cakes and puddings were baking because they would go flat. It must have been hard work, but they loved it and always got well-deserved praise for their spreads.

At tea time, Mam came into the front room to say that she had laid some food out on the table and we could help ourselves as we wanted. That's how it would be for the next couple of days; she had laid enough out for our tea and supper and the rest would come out of hiding for tomorrow's party. I had the rest of my chicken leg, including thigh, and Mam would always cut me a thick slice of cooked ham that she got every year.

I loved that at Christmas time: helping myself whenever I wanted to. There were fruit and nuts in bowls all over the house. To me it was sheer heaven, as I had got used to tight rationing. There was little choice of food, and fruit was only apples, pears, blackberries, gooseberries and the likes, when lucky.

I think I even felt guilty for being so lucky, but that did not stop me from pigging out. I always loved my food and this has never changed. I was allowed to eat it on the floor in the front room. Mam and Alma joined me and we listened to the wireless.

Dad stayed in the living room; he was writing notes onto small, carefully cut slips of paper and I was not allowed to see. I would know tomorrow at the party, and I was not to mention anything about it to the other children because it would be a surprise for all of them including me. So, I promised not to say anything about what I didn't know about anyway, and even Alma didn't know what the surprise was as she was also included in the game.

It was something else to look forward to the following day. It's funny how these daft little things make a Christmas so great. I even enjoy writing about it all these years later.

28

Next morning (Boxing Day), Mam came into my bedroom quite early and woke me up with a bacon butty and a cup of tea on a round tin pub tray. She said, 'Have a lay in if you want to and play with your things up here as we are busy downstairs.'

Shortly after she was back with a metal bucket containing cold water and a kettle of hot water plus soap and towel. She then told me to wash upstairs today and to use the chamber pot now if I needed a wee.

In each bedroom we had a bowl and a water jug. My room had a small table and, on the top, was always a china water jug standing inside a matching round bowl. The table had a long towel rail at one end with two hooks fixed to the opposite side end. So Mam poured some of the cold water that was already in the jug into the bowl, then added some hot water from the kettle and placed the jug next to the bowl on top of a lace mat that ran along the top of the highly polished sideboard table. The chamber pot was then pulled out from under the bed and emptied with care into the bucket, then pushed back under the bed after pouring some cold water to help dilute the odour from your wee. The "po" as we called them had to be scalded out once a week with domestic caustic soda. I had to pay attention to this, as it was to be one of my new chores next year, to do my own (no probs).

About midday, my cousin, Terry, turned up with his bag of presents that he had bought for relations when we both went shopping and it was placed under the tree until party time.

Meanwhile, Mam did not want us hanging around inside the house, so she gave us some fruit and sweets and told us to go out and play, but don't get dirty. So, after showing him my presents we went outside.

Most of my street pals were about; a couple of them had seen my cousin Terry before and were a bit wary of him because he was older than us. He lived in Napier Street, which is a back street running parallel to Uxbridge Street, but at the other end from Dale Street. It was a rough area and people always seemed to have their front doors open ready to pull you inside and eat you as you ran by.

I actually loved the street and all of the mad people who lived in it, especially my cousins, Derek and Terry, Aunty Tess and the old sod, Uncle Tom. I got to know most of the people in the street. It had a corner pub in it called the Napier Arms, and nothing else except houses, so there was no reason to be on the street as a stranger.

Anyway, we shared our goodies with my lot, and walked down to Meller's garden where we had a camp. Then we went to hang around the two shops and the off-licence until Alma called us in for party time. We were given a glass of pop and told to help ourselves to food from the massive spread but not to overdo it because there was trifle, jelly and Christmas cake all coming up later (literally in my case).

Aunty Nelly and Uncle Jack had arrived. I always felt a special warmth towards them - I don't know why. I think that Aunty Flo noticed this, because she said to me once that I should not call her Aunty Nelly as she was not my real aunt.

That did not make any difference to me; they were still and always were my aunty and uncle. We did not see them very often and they were staying overnight as they usually did on their rare visits. I don't know where they lived but she had a strong Brummy accent. They were great with kids and everyone loved Aunty Nelly. I asked Mam about Jack and Nelly at a much later date and a more appropriate time, and she told me that Auntie Nelly and Uncle Jack had no family of their own and couldn't have any children. They lived with us for a while when they first got together, but I would be too young to remember (maybe so but not too young to pick up on my instincts).

Everyone was trickling in now. Grandma was there with Auntie Evelyn and her children who lived with Grandad and Grandma at this time. I am not sure if Uncle Bill was on leave or not, but he would have been there if he was. They had three children by now: Pru, Billy-Boy, and baby Shirley.

Auntie Edie and my Mam were close sisters and Uncle Bill and Dad were close brothers, and it would be one of their rare times that they would meet up with their sister, Aunty Mabel, who would come from Stoke-on-Trent with her husband Uncle Arthur. He worked in the potteries. He was a nice bloke and easy to talk to and I loved his accent. They were a good couple and had two boys who were more spoilt than I was.

Uncle Phil Skivington with his pretty on-off girlfriend, whose name I cannot remember, were also there. She often used to serve me at her mother's shop that was just along the opposite side of Dale Street. I liked her. She was young and pretty and we got on well, but I always went shy if she singled me out. I think I was starting to notice girls. She had a finger missing; she had caught it in the mangle as a child, quite a common thing in those days.

So, the house was bursting with people, floor room only for kids. A lot of friends would call in to say a quick hello on their way to other places, which was good for the main family regarding space. So, it was now late afternoon and we were all stuffed with food with plenty more to be had.

Mam made an announcement that there would be a treasure hunt for the children devised by Uncle Albert. Alma looked at me, smiled and said, - 'the secret' - then we were each given a paper bag with our names on it and a piece of coloured wool. Starting with the youngest first and then one at a time you would have to find the next piece of wool by following the clue written on the rolled-up slip of paper on each separate piece of wool that you found. Your main little gift would be with the fifth piece of wool. The plan was your first piece of wool that was in your paper bag had a slip of paper with it, and on that was written a short rhyme giving a clue as to where your next piece of wool was hidden (things like "don't fall off the tree" or "hickory, dickory dock"). Dad would try and print them to suit the age of the searcher, plus each time you found the next required number of your wool leading up to number five, you would also find a small treat with it like a sweet or anything appropriate.

It was a great game and became a must at every big family party. Even the grown-ups loved to help the kids find the gifts, and my Dad would just sit there as though it was all nothing to do with him, but loving it.

After that, cousin Terry and I would give out our presents to close family members to much applause and commendation on our joint wisdom in choosing the ideal gifts for them.

We were then awarded a small glass of sherry each, and that was our start to ruin, as later we were both nicking drinks off the table and pouring them into our pop beakers. We then opened all the presents from underneath the tree and it was like Christmas morning all over again. As people had arrived, they had been putting presents under the tree for each other. Alma and I still had a present each from Mam and Dad. Mine was a Fair-Isle cardigan and, to my surprise, I liked it - I was beginning to like clothes. There were also other gifts for me from the relatives. I had far too much this year and I knew it, and I never forgot how poor some of my best friends were.

It was getting late now, and Uncle Tom had turned up, so they sat him in a chair and loosened his collar and tried to give him some water, but he already had a bottle of beer in his pocket.

I can remember Terry and I spending some time under the table eating and laughing at the grown-ups having a good time. Aunty Flo bruised her knee trying to fly through the front room doorway. Uncle Charlie's teeth came out when doing his *Nat King Cole* impression, but he was a very good singer and had no teeth of his own. He was the youngest of my Mam's siblings. Terry and I were just giggling at everything. I think we were both getting a bit happy and the punch bowl, which we were allowed, kept being topped up and, I think, got a bit stronger.

I don't remember going to bed; the last thing I do recall was being sick underneath the lilac tree. I woke up next morning in the small bedroom on my own. It was late morning and I felt as right as rain and raring to go. "Oh, to be young". So, I went downstairs in my pyjamas because I was in Alma's room and had no other clothes.

My bedroom door was closed plus I knew that Uncle Jack and Aunty Nelly were staying over. When I got downstairs I was not surprised to see it was all tidy and straight. Everyone had gone, except Uncle Jack and Aunty Nelly, who were sitting at the table chatting with Mam and Alma with a pot of tea, including one for me.

Uncle and Aunty were just about to leave for the train station and they kissed me goodbye as Mam told me to go back into my room now, put on my play clothes while she did some breakfast. Mam and Alma wanted me out of the way, as they still had things to do and put away. That suited me, as a couple of mates had already called for me. So, that was pretty much Christmas 1945. Other things would be going on between now and the New Year, like a get-together for close family at Grandma and Grandad's, and visits to and from close friends. During the festive season people would make a point of being in touch.

New Year was not a big deal in those days, except in Scotland where New Year was a bigger celebration than Christmas. I proved the point many years later when I spent a New Year in "Old Reekie" (Edinburgh) and lost over two days of my life.

Back in old Burton, New Year's Eve and New Year's Day were not a holiday period for workers. The Christmas holiday was only

Christmas Day and Boxing Day. But I was still a kid and every day was a holiday for me, with my street mates and the whole family, now that the war was over.

29

Because I was getting older, I now understood more about my family and the things they talked about, like how lucky we were not to lose any member during the war, especially as all the boys saw action except Charlie, who went directly from school into his local coal mine and would probably have been too young anyway.

For me it was a great winter holiday. We always celebrated New Year, but quietly, and we would always have gone to church a couple of times during that holiday.

I was still going to Sunday school, which was a bit boring, and I hated singing. Not only was I shy, but I only had a range of about four notes. I mentioned this at the dinner table one Sunday after school and my Dad started to laugh; then Mam said to him, laughing herself, are you going to tell him or shall I? She then took over, as she would, and told us the story about when my Dad joined the Coton church choir. He was singing so flat with no range, but he thought he was okay as he was tone deaf. He was ruining the choir, so when he turned up the following week, the vicar said to him, 'Young Thomas, you are so big and strong,' which he was,

'Would you mind pumping the organ for us on Sundays as we need someone just like you.'

Dad was chuffed - it was a man's job. We were all laughing, and that was one of their childhood stories that Alma and I would always ask them to repeat when reminiscing their younger days.

Mam and Dad seemed to get along well. They did not show a lot of close affection toward each other openly, but neither did any other married couples that I knew. They used to go to bed together on most Sunday afternoons until tea time and I would go out, weather permitting. My mates would be the same with their elders in bed or sleeping, and we would not be noisy if we were around houses. Sunday was a day of rest and adhered to by law - no DIY. You would even be frowned on if you cut the grass on your front lawn (should you have one) with a hand mower.

Dad worked hard as a driver. He would come home, have his dinner, sit in his chair and read the Daily Mirror newspaper, which we had delivered every day. He would then try not to fall asleep sometimes whilst reading. If he had not placed the paper over his face himself, then Mam would do it for him. We used to laugh at the way the paper fluttered when he breathed out. Sometimes, if he started snoring, Mam used to hold his nostrils together through the newspaper, which was easy, as we all have big noses in our family. We would fall around laughing, and if he ever woke up, he would take it in his stride and see the funny side. He was good like that, and he would often wake himself up with a start.

I never saw him get really angry with anyone. He would have flashes of anger, but they were mostly reserved for himself.

Everyone was trying to get their lives back in order, but there were so many adjustments to make. Factories that were making products for war would now, in most cases, convert back to civilian demands. A lot of women had learned highly skilled jobs and were equal to men and wanted to continue working whilst men were coming out of the forces and looking for jobs. The war had done what it always does and left us broke, so we had to take a big loan from the Americans to get started again.

Most of my Dad's loads were for building sites, and mostly roof tiles as the Marley Tile Company was in Burton and next to his depot: West Midland Road Services in

Branston Road. He said that most times the tiles were still warm when loading them.

He used to take me with him sometimes if I was on a school holiday and he was doing a short run like Leamington, Sheffield or Nottingham. Mam used to give us a packed lunch with big doorstep sandwiches, just like Dad always took, with a flask of tea. Coffee was rare back then in Britain and came in a glass four-sided bottle with a metal screw top. It was called Camp coffee, and it was a liquid that you would dilute with hot water. The only other coffee that I remember was proper ground coffee that Mam would make on a Sunday morning in a percolator.

I used to love these trips with my Dad; it was about the only thing we ever did when there were just the two of us out of the house. I used to pretend I was a driver's mate and we were delivering this important load to a secret location where we would meet up with a group of men who would help my driver unload the lorry as quickly as possible. I would stay in the cab, as instructed, as main look-out man.

Dad always seemed to know the men on the sites that he took me to, as they would call him Tom on arrival. I noticed that he was not shy when doing his job or with a group of men. Sometimes he would call in at another location to bring something back to Burton, but usually, with me, we would come back empty.

Even though he would always sweep the back of the lorry and the side and tail boards, the amount of dust that bounced off was surprising.

So, now we headed for home, but not before one more stop - the transport café for a wee and a proper mug of tea in a pint enamel mug like in the Army. I grew to love the smell and earthy atmosphere of those great little and big grease-ups, and then it was home in what had become an old bone-shaker now that it was empty. We were laughing and shouting at each other to be heard over the noise of the empty truck and this great big engine between us like a big table with a blanket over the top to muffle the sound and hold in the heat on a cold day, as the engine was the only form of heating.

It was on one of these trips with my Dad that we took a delivery to Nottingham. We pulled into a lay-by on the edge of Sherwood Forest to have a break, eat our sandwiches and drink the flask of tea. We would climb out of the cab to stretch our legs, and there were other people parked along the lay-by: cars, lorries, etc. Some folks would picnic on the edge of the forest. We sat on a log near the lorry that had a small "return load" on it and an open back.

I had a little look around. Dad said, 'What are you looking for - arrows?'

I just laughed. He knew I loved the Robin Hood era and I was hoping I might find a piece of branch to make a new bow with, but no luck. What I did find, though, was a new pack of cigarettes with one missing on top of a tree log near ours; so I went up to Dad, who was just finishing his Woodbine cigarette before driving on, and I said, 'I didn't find any old arrows but I did find these,' as I handed him the new ten-pack of Park Drive, less one.

He smiled and said, 'Well done, I like those cigarettes.' Then off we went home to Dale Street.

Another great day with my Dad: He used to drop me off home first, have a cuppa and then go to his depot to park up, and I would go out to play. I don't think there was any problem with passengers in those days; it would have been left to the discretion of the driver. I know that many drivers would take their wives with them for the day, especially if the delivery was to the seaside, or they would pick up hitchhikers (especially squaddies) for company or to help someone.

Back at school, we were in the run-up to the Easter holidays, 1946. Around this time of year, a local photographer would come to our school, and set up a backcloth and chair in the main hall. We would be filed in a class at a time and then, one at a time, to have a mug shot taken. I always hated it and I remember this one so well. I had been getting into lots of fights and tumbles, so my glasses were in bad shape. They were wonky with sticking plaster on the bridge and on one corner where the arm joins up with the lens frame. My hair would never behave and looked like Boris Johnson's on a bad day - and it was the same colour as I was turning from blond hair to fair.

The teacher even asked me if I wanted to remove my glasses for the picture. I said 'no, thank you,' because when I took off my specs, my left eye would move across into the corner in order to focus, and that made me look gimper than ever. It was not neglect on my folks' part. I was always getting new specs. I just kept breaking them, plus we did not have the NHS then.

So, as we all stood in line to have our mug shots done, we were all trying to tidy ourselves up a bit, especially the girls. I would borrow Christine's comb sometimes.

So, after that ordeal was over, so I thought, it was to get worse.

The following week we were all given two identical photos of ourselves on one sheet for free, with a printed list of prices and sizes for repeats and to send money with order. Each one was about two inches square. So, we all took them home. I wanted to throw mine away, but I knew that I wouldn't get away with it, so I gave Mam the envelope. She started laughing and, when she showed my Dad, he thought that it was pretty funny too. As for my big Sis, as soon as she saw it, exclaimed, 'I want one of those.'

So I was mortified when Mam gave me this order for more in an envelope with the money. The teacher opened it, looked at me and smiled; (and thought to himself, your folks must really love you).

Mam bought a whole sheet of the small ones and used to cut them off one at a time with her dress-making scissors and give them out, one at a time, as if they were a Penny Black stamp.

This last little story reminds me of an incident that happened many years later. So I will fast forward briefly to a time when I was living with one of my ready-made families, which consisted of a beautiful wife, three great kids, a cat called Smokey and a dog called Ben. Ben was such a handsome son of a dog that I got his portrait painted by a real artist. It was perfect, and when I took the picture home I shouted, 'I've got Ben's picture.' We all crowded into the lounge for the unveiling. I stood it on the floor as it was quite big, about two feet high, eighteen inches wide and framed. As I took off the brown paper covering, everyone went 'Aaah', except Ben who ran up to it, stopping short and kept barking at it. It was hilarious, and I thought to myself, 'poor Ben I know where you are coming from.'

I must try to obtain a copy of these old pictures, as to put them on show now would not bother either of us. We had a camera at home. I think it was called a Brownie box camera, and you would only see them at special events and holidays. The pictures were always black and white, the only coloured ones were tinted and that made them look worse. Even the black and white ones used to fade and go brown. It was all too much, unless one was an enthusiast.

I did take up developing a few years later to help my science teacher develop the school journey prints and get me out of all the lessons that I did not like (and so shooting myself in the foot).

My memories on the run-up to Easter and my birthday are not clear, probably because I was so busy having fun, one day would flow into the next. I had new roller skates for my birthday, plus a party at Grandma's on Broadway Street, where we would all meet up for regular family get-togethers. At Grandma's they would clear a space in the middle of the small front room to teach each other the Jitterbug. It was the latest dance from America, but we usually finished up doing the Charleston.

Aunty Tess would be the best one, as she used to be a professional dancer, but she was a bit shy in a crowd.

Dancing was very popular and, after the war, local town bands started getting bigger and bigger as they tried to copy Glen Miller and all the other big American bands with their music and singers. America led the way in Pop Music for many years to come and the local Saturday night dance would be the place to be, where the girls would go and wait whilst the boys had some Dutch Courage before going to find them. It didn't look worth it to me.

Poor Uncles Charlie and Phil; they were the youngest of the brothers and were always getting their hearts broken. They would have to go out on their own, get drunk, and then start all over again. So, by observing my own kinfolk as a youngster I learned - not a lot.

I was still doing my Saturday firewood collection, but sometimes my mate, Peter, would have to work on with his Saturday job delivering shoes. That did not bother me as I would just put it all in our coal house as stock and not bother doing the round on my own. Our regulars knew we were a bit hit-and-miss, but they always wanted firewood kindling when we had it, even through the summer months, so that they could stock up whilst the going was good. Most still had to fire up their copper boilers for hot water for baths, the dolly tub, etc.

Also, at the woodworking factory, I was always on the lookout for nice clean pieces of birch (whitish) plywood and other useful bits of wood so that I could make things with my hobbies tool kit. So, I didn't mind going to fetch the wood at all, weather permitting, and Betty loved it.

Model making became one of my favourite, I could say passions, as I would sit at my school desk staring out of the window, wondering whether to have square or round turrets on the fort I was making.

Some Events of interest during 1946 in the UK.

1st Jan – The first international flight from London Heathrow Airport, to Buenos Aires. – Atomic Energy Research Establishment founded at Harwell, near Oxford.

10th Jan – First United Nations General Assembly convenes at Methodist Central Hall Westminster.

17th Jan – the United Nations Security Council holds its first meeting at Church House in London.

14th Feb – the Bank of England is nationalised.

15th Feb – American dance craze, the Jitterbug, sweeps Britain.

20th Feb – Royal Opera House in Covent Garden re-opens after the War with The Royal Ballet (relocated from Sadler's Wells Theatre) performing *The Sleeping Beauty*.

5th March – Winston Churchill delivers his "Iron Curtain" speech at Westminster College in Fulton, Missouri, United Sates.

9th March – Stadium disaster at Bolton Wanderers' Burnden Park, Bolton, England; 33 killed and hundreds injured.

10th March – British troops begin withdrawal from Lebanon.

15th March – Labour Prime Minister Clement Attlee announces that Britain is granting India's wish for independence.

27th April – The first post-war FA Cup final is won by Derby County, who beat Charlton Athletic 4–1 at Wembley Stadium.

30

I was having lots of fun this year with my street mates and the gang. One day, after playing in the woods at the Ox Hay, Peter Sparrow and I decided to come home the other way as we both wanted a drink of water from what was called the Cherry Orchard that was at the top end of the Ox Hay playing field. As I recall there was no orchard there; perhaps it once was an orchard but in '46 it was a small park with seats, flowers, swings, and a real drinking well with nice cold Trent spring water, which I have previously referred to in my story.

So, after we'd had a drink, we continued out of the Cherry Orchard Park onto a footpath alongside the river Trent. With the river on our left we would walk along the wide path to get to an iron suspended bridge to cross the river to get into town. The river was quite wide at this point and the current could be fast as it widened along the way towards the main Trent Bridge, one of the major roadways in and out of town.

But, as soon as we came out of the Cherry Orchard, Peter said, 'Look at all the nuts on that tree.'

To which I said, 'What nuts?'

He said, 'Hazelnuts.'

I thought they looked like green unripe plums to me, but Peter knew about these things, and we decided to help ourselves. The trees were situated between the footpath and the river. It was late afternoon and very quiet. Peter was up the tree chucking down nuts. I was on the ground stuffing them inside my jumper, which was also on the ground, and inside my shirt.

I said to Pete, 'Come on down while the going is good.' So he started climbing down; then suddenly a man's voice shouted 'Oi' - it was the park keeper.

So, I picked up my jumper full of nuts and ran. I didn't stop moving or turn around until I got home, and I didn't drop a single nut.

I went in through the back door, still panting and out of breath. Mam and Dad were on their own in the back living room. After I had told them the story, Mam said to me, 'You ran away and left Peter up the tree.' Dad was shaking his head from side to side.

'Did the keeper nab him?' she asked,

I said, 'I don't know, I didn't turn around. I was just hoping that he would jump down without any nuts and follow me,' as I was just realising what a cowardly thing it was to do and to not even stop to wait for him along the way.

I put the nuts on the hearth rug and Mam went into the kitchen to get a large mixing bowl to put them in to ripen. Mam and Dad knew about these things, being country folk.

As Mam and I were filling up the bowl, there was a tap on the door. Dad said, "police" with a straight face, and I dropped another nut. Mam laughed as she went to the door.

It was Peter with a big bag of nuts. Then we got his side of the event. He said that he told me to run, knowing that he would catch up with me once out of the tree and footloose, and that I did the right thing 'cos we would at least have some nuts.

But, when he jumped down, the keeper said, 'Don't run off, I only want to chat.' So Peter stayed, knowing that he could run off at any time if he wanted to, but not wanting to push his probation order too far, and the keeper already knew our faces.

The keeper said that he didn't mind us taking windfalls but we were not allowed to climb the trees in the parks or along the river banks because of damage to trees, and people who have fallen into the river - some had even drowned.

'You've got all the trees in the Ox Hay woods to climb and swing on and your camp in there.'

Anyway, he gave Peter a big litter carry bag and said, 'No point wasting good nuts; put them in this bag and off you go to join your mate.'

So, we all had a good laugh of relief, a pot of tea and some of Mam's small cakes. Then Pete went home with his share of nuts and some cakes for his beloved Mum.

Next day, Peter told me that the keeper had been trying to pin us two down for a while as he was worried about us walking the bridge.

He said, 'I have watched you do it but too far away to nab you and daren't shout in case I make you jump and fall. There are long spikes at both ends to stop anyone from getting onto the top iron bands, and you are the only two people I have seen do it. I don't want anybody else to see you do it and be daft enough to try it, plus I would take some blame for not doing my job as park keeper if anyone fell, so will you please not do it any more.' And so we didn't.

Just as well; not only that it was often a fast current with whirlpools, but muddy and lots of rubbish thrown into the water from the bridge. Even a strong swimmer wouldn't want to jump in there. We got to know the keeper after that. We used to shout "hello" to him and he would wag his finger at us jokingly.

In our home, we were having a spring clean, as were many other homes following the end of the war. The shops were busy stocking up with paints and new wallpapers. The house decorating was always done by Mam. Dad did not interfere in any way, although I do remember him showing her how to use his plumb bob for hanging wallpaper. She mostly would start from a door frame and follow it all the way round the room. She had a good eye and always turned out a good job.

I don't think Dad liked decorating much and, if my scooter is anything to go by (still going strong, but still staining you with some green army paint on a warm day), he was more into making or constructing something.

The first room to be done and wallpapered was the small back bedroom over the large drive-in entry. It was decided that now Alma was a prefect high school teenager, whilst I was becoming more independent, that we should swap rooms. I agreed as I suddenly liked the idea of privacy. My own little space in our home; no more sleepovers with relations and silly girls.

My front bedroom was never private, as Alma already had her main wardrobe in it.

Sometimes I would come home, and she would have some of her mates in there, chatting and trying on clothes and hair styles. I did not mind this at all as I actually liked all of her friends and we all got on well. However, it was only a matter of time, and the swap over would be inevitable. My big sis would probably enjoy the drunken Saturday night conversations coming from our entry gates below more than me.

I think Alma stayed at Aunty Flo's or Grandma's (both handy for her school) whilst Mam got on with the room. She said to me, 'No firewood. Saturday you will be moving into your new room.'

Sure enough, when I got home from school next day, she said, 'You can sleep in your new room tonight, come and inspect it (jokingly).' So up we went. It was nice and light, even had new lino and a home-made woollen rug. It smelt a bit fresh because it was not properly dry yet - but it was not an unpleasant smell, and new lino always smelt for a while. I wouldn't dare complain as I knew she was chuffed with it, and I would have got a clout for sure. The bigger I got, the harder her clouts came. She clouted me a lot when I deserved it, but she knew me well, so it would be a clout in passing - not stand there so I can give you a slap or stand there and tell me off because that would always make me cry, whatever age.

Dad gave me corporal punishment once in my life, and that little story is not far away. Alma was a different kettle altogether. She had a wild dominating temper and played "Jekyll and Hyde" better than anyone I ever met. She seemed to be mellowing of late; maybe she was going through that awkward stage of changing from girl to whatever, or maybe she knew about my fighting and getting bigger and stronger and that the worm might turn, or maybe pigs might fly. Either way my big sis and I never ever did have a big fall out - at least, not to my knowledge.

Saturday morning - I woke up in my new bedroom. I would have slept well, as I always did. Mam had already moved my stuff into a large built-in corner cupboard on the left end wall of the entrance door. The right-hand wall of the door was the wall between Mam and Dad's room and mine. The outer wall had a nice Georgian window with two opening side light sashes, about three feet square in all, where I would look out over onto the big back yard to see all kinds of activities to do with cattle, etc. I thought, I am going to enjoy my little room (and I did), but my immediate problem was that I had to sort out my bits and pieces. I had been told to dwindle things down so that I could fit in all my stuff - all of my toys put away and nothing lying around. I was told I had a lot of stuff that could be thrown and given away and that now was a good time as I was getting to be a big boy.

So, knowing I had no choice, I started by moving in my latest popular things and, considering that Christmas and my birthday had just passed, I had even more. The corner cupboard had a hat shelf with a hanging rail attached to the underside, which was for clothes only. The bottom of the cupboard had a well, so it was like a big box that I could use. Also in my new room was a chest of three drawers with a mirror and washbowl on the top, and I was allowed the bottom drawer for my bits and pieces plus a wall shelf that Alma used to keep her books on. I was surprised how much I managed to contain once I got started, especially after Dad told me that when he was on the move in the Army, they would have to carry all their worldly goods with them, and even on camp they would be lucky if they got a locker or a trunk.

There was one thing that I could not throw away and that was my old Teddy. He was threadbare, dog eared, had no fur on his chest, his right eye was hanging down his right cheek by a piece of thread, looking like a shiny marble conker. I hid him underneath some comics and would have given him to someone I liked but he was too far gone, and I didn't want him just thrown away. I know that he was just a small bag of stuffed wadding, but he had been my friend forever. I don't even know where he came from, I just know that we cuddled up together every night, went through a war together, and sat under the table and the stairs with a candle during night air raids. I've even taken him into the air raid shelters, but now I was too big for such things, so I would just keep him hidden in the cupboard.

After throwing away some useless stuff, I put other things that I could live without into an orange box and carried it down to Meller's garden. We still had a so-called camp there, and I wanted to share things with the gang: stuff like American comics as I only liked Superman now, because I preferred the characters in the British comics. Also a humming top made of tin which was shaped like a flying saucer. You would hold it on solid ground, the base was dish shaped with a hard tip in the centre for spinning on. Then, you would pump the handle on the top, like a blow lamp of that time, to make it spin round. The harder and faster you pumped, the faster and longer it would spin for after letting it go. They would be painted different bright-coloured patterns that would change like a kaleidoscope as it slowed down as would its humming sound too: great fun. I gave that to Cecil Taylor's little sister. "Whips and tops" only seemed to be in the shops around Pancake day and were considered bad luck to play with after the month of April each year. I don't know why, but they could be quite dangerous.

Whilst sorting out my junk, I noticed my casting block for making lead soldiers, about the size of a church bible, so I took it to school to show the old Captain. I was always comfortable with him, and although he was not our form teacher any more I still did drawings and printing for him. We would also have him for some lessons, like history, and he always seemed to be the one who filled in for other teachers or, if there was a spare lesson, it would be him with one of his wonderful stories. He seemed to be like a deputy head.

Anyway, it turned out that other school kids also had casts. We would bring them into school for a special lesson and the Captain asked us all in our class to bring in any bits of scrap lead or broken lead toys so that they could all be put into a melting pot, that the school would provide, and that we would have a lesson making new lead pieces with whatever castings we brought in, under his supervision. So, we all took in our broken bits of lead and we soon had enough for the following week's lesson.

On the day in question, we went into class. The Captain was all set up with a table and on it was a gas ring or Bunsen burner, and a large empty hot glue pot that fitted into its own water kettle. So, we all sat at our desks and watched him fire up the small gas ring. Then he put on the round glue kettle that had a wire bucket type handle on it. He told us all to gather around him and he placed the iron glue pot that fitted exactly into the top of the metal kettle. He then put in as many small pieces of lead as he could, talking to us all the time.

At this point we were told to return to our seats and, whilst we waited for the lead to melt, he talked about early castings that were made of all sorts of things from sand to iron, to make cannon balls, weapons and so on. Each time the lead had melted he would pour it into the casts that we had brought. There were three or four and when they were hard enough he would open the two sides. Then we could get involved by breaking off the strands of lead from around the edges and where the lead was poured in from the top. Then we would put these bits on his table to go straight back in the pot for re-melting. It went well and we all ended up with a couple of pieces each.

I was surprised how clean and shiny they looked, like silver, although they soon would fade. They would normally get trimmed, filed and painted. We had Cowboys, Indians, soldiers, farm animals, cows smaller than sheep, but it didn't matter - they were toys. It was a great fun day and full of learning, all highly illegal today.

The next significant school day that I remember was the last day of this term pending the summer break. It was called a free day. We had to turn up at school as usual, but we were allowed to dress as we liked and take in something to play with, like quiet board games and books. We boys thought it was so funny when the girls turned up in their groups wearing make-up and their Mam's shoes, but we also commented amongst ourselves how much older they looked, as we realised that we too were growing up.

On that day we were also encouraged to go out into the playground and mix with each other, using some folding tables and chairs that had been set up by the caretaker, who took charge and was on parade for the kids outside. As it was a sunny day, the classroom doors were left ajar so that we could go in and out in an orderly fashion as we liked. The teachers spent most of the time in the main hall and staff room having a meeting.

After dinner the afternoon register was called; then we were told to line up in our usual place outside in the play yard carrying our stuff or put it on the tables that were still outside. The teachers lined up and the Head Mistress said a few words and ended by shouting 'Have a happy holiday, see you next term' - to which we all cheered, as if we had just been released early from prison, when, in actual fact, we were all enjoying ourselves as if at a party (talk about brain wash).

Anyhow this was the start of a great summer holiday for me: lots of fun, mischief, and trouble. My first adventure was that I and three other members of my clique decided that we would go to a place called Tutbury, a small market town about ten miles from Burton. None of us had been there, but it had an old castle. So, as we were all into Robin Hood and Knights of Old, we wanted to go and see it.

We got together a small kitty and we would get our Mams to give us a packed lunch. We went to the railway station and got on a train, affectionately called the "Tutbury Jinny" that used to do a shuttle service all day long between Burton and Tutbury. I also seem to remember that it went forward one way and backwards t'other. It was a wonderful old steam engine. People used to commute on it every day to work at the Breweries, etc. I believe this service ran until the 1960s.

The fare was quite cheap in 1946. So, off we went to conquer and capture all at this Tutbury Castle. We had an army shoulder bag, a flat-ish shaped army water bottle full of cold water, two bottles of pop: one of lemonade and one of dandelion and burdock, loads of salad, sandwiches and fruit, and off we went with strict orders to behave ourselves and keep out of mischief (yeah, right).

No trouble at the station, we all had a pee there as we knew that once on the train there was no toilet and once you got into the carriage that was it - not even a corridor. That was normal back then and we only had one stop to go, and we were happy. It was so good to be on a train with my mates in our own carriage instead of trying to write down their numbers as they whizzed by.

We were in good spirits as we shared our own carriage and a bag of sweets we had bought at Burton station when we got our tickets. In no time at all we were pulling into Tutbury station. The carriage doors can only be opened from the outside. We already had the window down as it could be operated from the inside by passengers. By pulling or lowering a strong leather strap with perforated holes, like on a waist belt, that you could clip it onto a fixed pin at whatever air gap you wanted. We were able to reach over to the outside handle and open the door. After the ticket collector had checked us out, we decided to keep hold of our own tickets in case any of us got lost or separated.

So, there we were outside Tutbury railway station without a clue of which way to go and half a brain between us, but it was a small place and we soon got some bearings. Tutbury has a lot of history, but none of us were much into that at the time; we were just on a fun "see what happens" day.

We found the Castle without any problems. It was mostly in ruins but there were still some bits standing, enough to make it interesting. The first thing we did after entering the grounds was climb up the banks or ramparts, find a nice place to sit, and eat all our sandwiches and pop. The castle looked out over the river Dove and, as we had our picnic, we chatted on a plan of what to do and we pretty much decided that we would just do the Castle today as the area was quite big. There was a tower and other bits still standing that we wanted to do, we also knew already that we would be tired going up and down these steep banks. None of us had been here or even to Tutbury before so it was a first. We knew about Mary, Queen of Scots, who was held at this castle for quite a while, not exactly chained up, but under guard and not allowed to go outside of the castle, by order of Queen Elizabeth 1st, before going to trial and the Tower of London.

The Castle and town had been almost destroyed and rebuilt following some revolution. So, we had a look around it all. I remember looking down from inside the top of the tower and thinking, *how could you escape from here*? and I was in awe of the size of the stones and walls and tried to imagine the different kinds of people who had stood on this spot before me. After we had done enough, I wanted a cup of tea from a tea stall that was there. I had grown to enjoy a nice cuppa in the afternoon, and to think that I used to hate tea.

On the way out from the Castle, we spotted a small barn. I am not sure whether it was part of the Castle grounds or not, or perhaps used to be, but inside it was full of bales of hay with a big pile of bouncy hay already on the floor, and no one around. We were playing fairly quietly to start with, but as we got more daring we would make more noise. We were jumping right off the top bales into the heap of straw below, playing cowboys and shooting each other off the top.

We were all inside the barn jumping around, then suddenly a man appeared in the doorway and just stood there. As we all got down and stood in front of him, we could have run off, but no one tried to, and my mates thought the same as me - where to and no harm done.

The man said that he was the farmer and that we were on his property. He was well spoken using plain English, a bit like a teacher; he seemed like a nice man. He explained how dangerous hay ricks can be when the bales tumble and how much damage we had done. Then he took our names and my address and school. Then, with a notebook and pencil that he had in his jacket pocket, he gave us each a signed note and made us promise that we would give it to our parents when we got home, and to tell them to deal with us the way they saw fit. Then he told us to keep out of mischief and not to forget as he pointed us to the big field gate.

On our way to the railway station, we were already laughing about it as we were picking the straw from our clothes prior to boarding the train back to Burton. We all still had our tickets and my Dad's shoulder bag. At Tutbury Station, Jinny was already at the platform, firing up to go. We managed to get an empty carriage again for the trip back to Burton. It was still afternoon and most passengers would be coming from Burton to Tutbury. On the train run, I told the others that I would tell my folks about the farmer and give them his note. I didn't see it as a big deal anyway, plus he had my address and school.

Gordon Adams and Reggie Wallis agreed to do the same, but Peter Sparrow screwed his up and threw it out of the train window, which was fair enough as his Mam would worry, and his Dad would probably clout him anyway if he found out that he'd had a fun day trip. So, we got off old Jinny at Burton Station and ambled our way home. We would have got an ice cream each or some sweets on the way. I know we were all hungry and tired. We separated at our respective homes.

As I went in through our back door, I pretended not to look too happy, because I was holding the farmer's note in my hand. After telling them that we had a great time, I said that we did get into a little bit of trouble and, after trying to explain the dialog between the farmer and us, I handed the note to my Dad who read it then handed it to Mam. I don't think Alma was in.

Then Dad gave me a lecture on how a farmer needed his hay and straw to take him through the winter months for feed and bedding for his animals and to sell some bales to make a living. I never heard him say so much in one go. He then said go and put your pyjamas on and come back down.

When I came back down, Dad was standing there with a slipper in his hand. He said, 'Bend over and hold the arm of the chair.'

So, I bent over; then he hit me with the sole of the slipper across my backside three times, and then said, 'Now go upstairs to bed without any tea.'

So, I just ran up the stairs and jumped into bed. I didn't cry because I realised that I had done wrong and was duly punished. Dad understood farming and hard work, and would never hurt me in any way, but he thought I was getting a bit out of hand lately and needed reining back a little.

That was to be the only time my Dad ever struck me in any form. A bit later on that evening, Mam came up to my room with my tea.

I said, 'Where is Dad?'

She said, 'Gone to his allotment.' (Yeah, right). So, I ate my tea and slept like a log after a good day and a good lesson learned.

31

It is summer school holiday time now, 1946. I am 9 years old and the Bertram Mills Big Top Circus is rolling into town.
It was the biggest circus I ever saw, with elephants, lions, horses, and many others, plus all of the performers and crew, with a small brass band in brightly dressed uniforms. I went to it with Mam. Dad didn't go, and Alma went with her mates. I loved the circus and everything about it and thought that I might run away one day to join one to become a great trapeze artist or a clown. This was the biggest circus in the country at the time, and I remembered seeing some of the acts before as this was my second time of going to the Bertram Mills Circus.

I had a romantic innocent view of a circus after watching my very first movie called *Dumbo*, a cartoon film about a flying elephant and, as Bertram Mills always had loads of elephants, I must have related some of the fun feeling from the movie to a real circus. I used to also think that all of the animals in the circus had a good life, with food and bedding and enjoyed performing in the ring, but I was to grow out of this and dislike the way that mankind has used and abused most animals, but it was great fun at the circus.

– 'An elephant story' –

When Bertram Mills took his circus to Scotland, he would camp on the edge of Loch Ness and he would have his elephants taken down and into the Loch for a splash around. One day, as they were crossing the water, they were holding onto the tail of the one in front with their trunks as trained to do and, as they got low in the water, a photographer in the distance spotted them and took a couple of pictures, thinking that they were one long humpy creature. This is how the legend of the Loch Ness Monster began.

I was going to Whitby again for ten days. The plan was that I would go with Alma and then Mam and Dad would join us for a week. I was so looking forward to this holiday and I said during one of our Sunday table chats that I wanted to go to the small Captain Cook Museum, and to see his statue and monument that were in Whitby.

Dad said, 'He didn't come from Whitby.'

I said, 'I know, but Whitby was where he fell in love with the sea and got a job in the Merchant Navy. He got a job as a deck hand before becoming a famous Captain.

Dad asked, 'How do you know this?' and I replied, 'Because we are doing explorers at school like Captain Cook, Cecil Rhodes and David Livingstone.'

Dad looked impressed, because I think he had my measure. He was aware that I was not too bright, always looking at comics, not books, and my writing was like a spider walking through ink across the page. Perhaps, he thought, there is hope for this kid yet. The truth is that I loved the way our history and geography lessons were put across like adventure stories. We would get a colouring-in paper with an outline drawing on it that we would colour in toward the end of our lesson and stick it in our exercise book.

So off I went on the train with my big sis to Whitby. It was very strange that the only times I ever really got on with my sister was when it was just the two of us, like no parents around, and this went on into adulthood.

So, we had a fun few days with her in charge. Alma could be very funny and had a wicked sense of humour and, now I was older, she did not have the same responsibility thrust upon her as during the war. I always thought that she would never be a good mother, but she proved me wrong in the end and, although I have always loved her, and always will, I never did trust her 100 per cent.

We went down to the beach most days. My little girl playmate from the house, Christine, would come with us. We had some rainy days, so I bought a model sailing ship that had to be put together, and a model aeroplane made of balsa wood. This had to be built and glued together with special quick drying glue, and then covered in a lightweight paper. You could paint it, stick on transfers, attach the big elastic band supplied to the back of the propeller to the inside of the plane, and try your luck, but not from the top of a cliff at Whitby.

I was allowed to do my model making on the lady's dining table. Mam and Dad joined us at the weekend. I think my Dad's army mate had his holiday time off his job at the same time, as the four of them did things together. I got to see Captain Cook's monument with Statue, and his Memorial museum, in Whitby.

Captain Cook was born in Middlesbrough into a farming family. He did not like farming and wanted only to go to sea. His father had a friend who owned a merchant shipping line and agreed to give young James an apprenticeship as a seaman, starting at the bottom as a deckhand. He became one of the world's greatest explorer navigators and the rest is history. The Memorial Museum is in Grape Lane, on the harbour side. Cook lodged there between 1771–72 after his first voyage.

During our holiday at Whitby, we also made a couple of trips along the coast to Scarborough and Filey, which I also loved because they were different. I think we got a special bus like the old private coach. We called them charabancs and I think the trip each way was less than one hour.

It was a great holiday until the day before we came home. When I came out of the bedroom after putting on my swimming trucks to join the others down at the beach, I was at the top of the stairs. They had a lovely highly polished handrail that finished with a carved wooden rope curl on top of the bottom newel post with a flat-ish top. If there was no one around I would slide down it. So, as it was quiet, I cocked my leg over and slid down as I had done a few times before. When I got to the bottom, I was sitting astride the newel cap and I stayed there with my tight trunks on, thinking that it felt nice. As I was sitting there, enjoying my new strange feelings I suddenly got another feeling. It was a whack across the backside with a rolled-up newspaper, delivered by the lady of the house.

She continued to walk past me and on into her kitchen without saying a word. I jumped off the banister and ran outside, not knowing which way to go, so I started walking downhill, thinking I should keep walking all the way and into the sea for being such a dirty little boy. I caught up with the others and just sat quiet most of the time dreading going back for tea.

Anyway, when we did go back for tea, nothing got said and to my knowledge never did, but I don't think that I ever looked the lady of the house in the face again.

Next day was the end of our holiday and we all said and kissed goodbye at the railway station and it seemed that I was forgiven as we then came home to Burton. I went straight out to play as I had some Scarborough rock for the gang.

During the summer holiday, I went off with my Dad in his lorry to other local towns a couple of times with his deliveries. He had started doing some loads to and from

Newcastle on Tyne, where he would stay over and come back the next day. It was around this time that Mam tried to persuade him to get in touch with his old Battery Commander, who had told him if you ever want a job after the war get in touch and you can have a good job in our family business. That was a coach company and, at the time, Dad was a sergeant driving instructor and his boss was this young Captain, who was in charge of the Regiment MT.

I think after getting back from our holiday that Mam was impressed with the coach drivers in their uniforms, hats and sunglasses, which seemed a lot better than overalls and a dusty lorry. Dad never wore a hat, only his demob trilby on his few outings. Mam was probably right, as people were into the idea of holidays, so coach firms were setting up all over the country. Also, holiday camps were on the way, and most civilians did not drive.

But I think Dad would have been too embarrassed to contact his officer and friend and feel that he was putting him on the spot, plus I think that he quite liked his job as he loved driving. He would sit at the table for hours with his maps, working out the best routes to different places all over the country. His map reading was spot on - that would be his Army training. I also noticed how neat his writing was. Even though Mam and Dad went to the same small country village school, they were both educated people and could read, write and spell very well.

Dad also was a bit of a loner and would love the freedom that came with the open road. Driving was different then, more fun and more interesting. No traffic jams, wave at just about everyone going the other way, and get held up behind the odd farmer by his hay rick, tractor, cows, sheep or horses. You also had to be a bit of a mechanic because breakdowns went with the job. Driving a lorry then was also tiring with a noisy engine shaking the cab around and no power steering to help when you are well loaded. You also had to double de-clutch on gear changes. There was no music, unless you sang to yourself so that you didn't nod off to sleep. He-he-he.

Mam took me swimming a couple of times to an open-air pool with a diving board. I remember it was hot and we took a picnic with us. It was free and run by the council and it was okay, but Mam didn't go in the water. I think it was mainly for kids, but it did have a deep end and a shallow end, where I stayed. I didn't take any mates, mainly because they could all swim, and I was embarrassed because I could beat them at most things. I was quite timid in the water and didn't care for the other kids that could swim. They kept splashing me when they dived in, screaming and shouting, so I would climb out to watch them with envy. What I really needed was a home with a private heated swimming pool.

Mam and I used to do a lot of things together - reason being that we shared a lot of interests. We liked all music, going to the pictures, anything to do with theatre, animals to which we both would talk in silly sounding voices that only animals can understand. Whereas Dad never wanted to go to the pictures, or even whistle a tune, let alone listen to one. I think Alma was the same, as she didn't go to piano lessons any more and would only lift the lid if I asked if I could have a go, which I was still not allowed.

Mam used to play it, though. She'd never had a lesson, but she was not too bad. Her left hand used to play almost the same bass accompaniment for every tune. That was okay as she would accompany herself as she sang whatever song was popular at the time and it would have been pretty much the same tempo. I used to love to hear her singing. She used to do Ann Shelton and Vera Lynn, as good as. Mam's side of the family were all musical, but Dad's side seemed not to be. Dad was into making things and gardening.

One day Mam took me to a live show. It was called *The Huggets*. I think it was only on for two performances at the Electric Theatre that was normally a cinema. The show was about a London family getting back to normal life after the war, all done in a light-hearted way, with a cast of four big stars of the day. Jack Warner was the husband and father, Kathleen Harrison was the wife and mother, Diana Dors was the eldest, "flirty" daughter, and Petula Clark was the "butter wouldn't melt" little schoolgirl. It was a great show, "well real" acting and so funny. I think it was a pilot show on tour, because I can remember it on radio and early TV and it may have had a different name when we saw it live in Burton.

The cast of that show:
Jack Warner: I had seen in British films and he went on to become best known as *Dixon of Dock Green*, in the TV series of the same name.
Kathleen Harrison: was and went on to be one of our best supporting actresses.

Diana Dors: went on to become a pin-up model and an underrated actress both in Britain and America.

Petula Clark: continued acting up until she made a hit record called "Downtown"; then became an international singing star and went to live in France with her new French husband.

Jack Warner had two sisters, called Elsie and Doris Waters and, at this time, they were more famous than Jack, as the whole country loved them as "Gert and Daisy" on the radio. I had the pleasure of meeting these lovely ladies years later in 1956, when they were top of the bill and I was an also-ran, but that will be part of my story when and if I get there. But, before slipping back, let's fast forward to the '70s. I carried out some maintenance building work on Diana Dors' home in Sunningdale, but never met her.

The gang and I were into bows and arrows again and, now we were growing up a bit, we were looking for stronger bows and better arrows for target practice as we didn't shoot at each other any more. We were experimenting with all kinds of tips for weight to make them stay in a tree and the like, and fletching. This was difficult with our limited resources, but we managed and had fun.

We also practised knife throwing at trees as most of us had knives. I had one like a miniature Bowie knife, with a leather handle and good balance. I always kept it very sharp as I would use it a lot as a tool - I loved whittling. That style of knife was popular, and you could get them in different sizes from most tool or hardware shops. Most people carried some kind of knife, if only a pen knife. I never heard or saw anyone get stabbed or cut in anger - only in the movies. Even in a punch-up, if your opposite went down you would wait for him to get back to his feet and then continue unless he held his hand up.

Kick boxing would have been well frowned on, as there were no martial arts in this country then. Even unarmed combat in the Forces was in its infancy, but we did have different styles of boxing and wrestling: staff fighting, sword fencing, etc. not to mention "Ecky Thump" and pie in the face.

Sometimes I would have to go to Dad's allotment to collect food stuff and take him tea and sandwiches. I would usually take Betty on these trips, with or without the barrow. Dad would have gone there straight from work on some light summer evenings. He kept his wooden gardening barrow that he made, of course, with his gardening tools in the lock-up shed that was on his plot. You could trust most people back then, plus they would look out for each other and check with any strangers near the plots. Sometimes he would sit in his deck chair smoking his pipe, and I would think to myself how boring is that? Ha, small kid - small mind.

I would take Betty out playing with us sometimes now that I was older and knew how to look after her. I would keep her on the lead and give her plenty of water. I used to carry a pocketful of dog biscuits, and even ate the odd one myself. This was after Mr Jack Leedham told me that they were wholesome as he popped one into his own mouth and chewed on it. He also once gave me a sweet that was really a small piece of soap then fell about laughing with a couple of his workmen as I spat it out on the yard. He then gave me a small bag of real sweets, as a peace offering, that I gave to my street mates; they seemed okay. I did see the funny side, and he knew that I was just as spoiled as his own son John. He would have got on well with my Uncle Tom.

Betty used to love it when she went with us to the Ox Hay, as I would let her off the lead and she would just race around like a mad thing, and could she run, she was so fast. Mam said that she was a Manchester Terrier crossed with a whippet. She was always very sharp and active and when you let her go it was as if she was born to run, even without chasing anything. Then she would run into the edge of the river to have a drink of Trent water. She was a lovely family dog, even if she did chew Teddy's ear when she was a pup.

Alma was out a lot with her mates which included boys. Tennis seemed to be her thing at the moment. Dad ordered a tennis racket for her from another town and one day when I was with him at work he parked up and told me that he would not be long. When he returned and climbed up into the cab, he was smiling and holding a tennis racket. He said, 'This is for your sister's birthday tomorrow.'

I gave him a smile of approval as we pulled away to continue home. He looked chuffed - I think that he had just done a good deal. He liked giving presents and I don't think that he ever had a lot of money for himself, plus everything to do with the allotment, like seeds, plants, tools, rent, etc. was all out of his own pocket money.

I think Mam was a bit unfair on him sometimes. Dad was a hardworking, proud man who just wanted an honest job and to do for his family, whereas Mam had ambition and drive, with a "go and get" nature, so sometimes there was a stubborn clash and, as usual, I could see both sides.

It was a good summer holiday and even great fun playing in the streets. The streets would be full of kids climbing lampposts, playing ball; even the grown-ups would join in sometimes for fun, as they remembered that we had also gone through a war in our way. We were also allowed to play on most bomb sites as long as they were reasonably safe. No Health and Safety rules then, and the street traffic was not a problem as there were few drivers. There were always kids and animals on the roads, horses and carts everywhere and they had right of way. You would also see plenty of Bluebottles (Coppers) on the beat walking, or on a bicycle, sometimes in pairs and wearing the round Bobby's hats. We didn't run away from them - no point as they knew us anyway, and they were okay. Sometimes we would chat to them.

On one occasion we had broken the top of a rotten fence coming out of a property of a disused house with a nice apple tree on our way back from the canal, and we were spotted and named. We had only just got back to Meller's garden when we spotted the police on our tail so all we could do was let the apples fall on to the ground from our shirts. The two of them came over the road onto Meller's waste ground. The older one said to his young sidekick, 'Oh look, windfalls,' as he pointed to the apples on the clay looking earth. I knew the older one and his name at that time; he was a good bloke.

He said, 'Gordon isn't it?'

I said, 'Yes, Sir.'

'If you are not running around shooting people, you are stealing their apples.'

I tried not to smile as I recalled that he once tracked me to my home last year, as it was reported to the police that a young kid was running around some scaffolding shooting a real pistol. I showed him my cap gun to which he said it would look and sound real in the dark.

So, he had a cuppa and a laugh with Mam as I had rushed home when someone told me that the police were looking for me. He then said that he would now go and tell the old lady who had reported it.

Needless to say, Mam had a field day with this one. So, regarding the apples theft, he said, 'Do you both want a clip or shall I see your parents?'

Pete and I said together, 'A clip please, Sir,'

So the older one gave us both a clip around the ear; then gave us a proper warning about private property. Then he bent down, picked up two nice apples, gave one to his young partner. They walked off, smiling and munching on their apples.

We were laughing as we put the apples in our camp to share around. Our coppers cared about people, and a London 'Bobby' was legendary all over the world.

The summer holidays of '46 were just about to end and I was preparing for the next term at school. It seemed a long time since I'd been at school, because I had done so much during the holiday and school was out of my mind until now. I was feeling quite scared to return as I didn't like school any more, knowing that the struggle to keep up would be harder, plus my Dad was home now and I didn't want him to know what a dunce I was, but I was never a coward and never bunked off, "played true ant" or said I was sick when not.

32

So, it is the first day back at school and I feel sick, but once I am in the playground I am okay.

I don't remember much about this term except that I was ducking and diving like before trying to cover myself only getting away with it because the teachers had class sizes of thirty or more and there were a few others like me. They had the syllabus to get through by the end of term and so would have to ignore real stragglers like me.

What I did work out, though, was that I could learn, but it just took me longer. Once I got it, I got it, but when I couldn't keep up due to my writing and day dreaming, I would lose the plot and give up. I didn't know that I had dyslexia as it did not exist then, and I was known as thick. I just did my best, but even copying off the board was slowing me more as I was left handed and we had started to do joined up letters on our words. We called it real writing, and we had to do this with an ink pen that you dipped into an ink pot and learn how much ink to put on your pen nib by practice. You then had to write onto your paper with the letters slanting to the right – an impossible task if you are left-handed without smudging your writing with your hand. And to do it with a pencil you have to hold your hand in an awkward position, either above or on your writing. There was no room or time for exceptions or differences. Learn to use your right hand I was told many times, but I always did the best I could and put up with it.

I suppose, if nothing else, I was learning how to cope when there was no choice.

I had the same problem with arithmetic, but the crazy thing is that I was good at getting the correct answer to most simple sums but could not show any working out on my page. I could do it in my head but I could not easily grasp the normal format of setting out a sum like long division, fractions, etc. However, once I understood the sum I could, most times, do it in my head and sometimes write down some numbers that I needed to carry over to complete a sum, but it was so unorthodox.

I was told to do it properly and stop cheating. Once I had to empty my pockets because I put down the correct figures to an addition then take-away, to a fraction sum and was accused of cheating off my friend Christine, who did help me sometimes. I was the only one with the correct answer but showing no workings, because the workings were on a picture inside my head of my Dad's wooden setting-out folding ruler, and I understood fractions to the inch or foot or yard. I just had to convert it into my sum, quite clever for a dunce, I thought. But no matter what school I was at, I never hit it off with the Maths and English teachers and it was to get worse as my schooldays progressed, or I should say continued.

I had started reading my first real book at home. It was the old classic *Black Beauty*, one of my Christmas presents. It was a good book with a hard cover and I put it on my new bookshelf with my other good books and annuals. I could read but was very slow and some words I couldn't manage, so I had to guess what they said or meant, which was frustrating as there was no flow to the story like when the old Captain read it. But if I didn't practise I would never learn, and I had learned pretty much how to read a comic. I read in my bedroom when I went to bed as it was still daylight at the time and earlier when at school. I could only manage one page a night, but it was a start. I found it hard to concentrate and that was one reason why I didn't want to read downstairs, plus I was embarrassed and so amazed at the speed of my sister's reading. I felt that I was losing ground at school and confidence, which was making me withdraw a little, yet I loved everything about school except me.

Beauty, my four-legged neighbour seemed happy that I had moved into my new small room overlooking his yard and I would make a point of opening the window to shout and give him or her a wave. I don't think I ever really knew whether Beauty was a boy or girl, but it didn't really matter, a friend is a friend.

All in all, '46 was a good year for me. Most of my mates were getting taller and I wasn't, but I was filling out and developing leg and arm muscles. Some kids called me fatty; it didn't bother me as I didn't have an ounce of fat on me, but because I was short and stocky I could look a bit plump when relaxed. The one that did get me into fights was when they called me "four eyes".

Winter was closing in and the dark cold nights were upon us. I still did the firewood run every Saturday, followed by the pictures and a bag of chips from New Street on the way home. I stayed indoors more this winter. I think that I liked the family unit now that Dad was home and Mam was not doing night shift any more.

We would all listen to the wireless in the living room with an open fire and a small supper. I would have a nice cup of cocoa before being the first one up to bed. I would hear Dad come up sometimes as I was reading my page, as he was normally up before 6am.

Bonfire night was good again on Meller's garden, with fireworks, and even Mam and Dad popped along for a while. I was now putting a little savings by so that I could go shopping again with my cousin Terry for family Christmas presents. My Dad had given up smoking so that he could also afford to buy some presents, that he had never done before. I was not too bad at saving a little money, but was starting from scratch, and I still owed some to Mam for a couple of things that I wanted to buy after I had spent my allowance from my Whitby holiday. So, I had to learn the lesson that you must pay back.

Then, when we got back, we had the Statutes Fair, and Guy Fawkes night, so I was skint and in debt and I was only nine years old.

Would things change? Tune in for the next chapter.

33

We are now on the run-up to Christmas 1946. Mam is busy doing her baking and cooking Christmas puddings, mince pies, organising meat, a large cooked ham, and also a large chicken for Christmas dinner.

My cousin Terry and I did our shopping early this year, so that we only had a few bits to get at the last minute when we had got more cash. The shops were even busier than last year, and we did most of our shopping in Woolworths, which was always the most popular shop at Christmas time. Mam decided to use the front room more this year and instead of a fir tree, she bought a holly tree and placed it on top of a built-in base cupboard next to the window and set into the fire breast recess. There was another matching cupboard on the other side of the fire breast. Each had a pair of opening panelled doors to blend with the house doors with a middle wooden shelf inside - a normal fitment of the day.

Mam said that a holly tree was a proper Christmas tree (so that was that). I did notice that most of our lovely trinkets did not go on the tree but lots of tinsel, bunting and crackers did.

Alma and I had our pillowcases in the front room this year, and it was better in a way: nice fire, more room and easy to keep tidy. I didn't ask if Santa was okay with this; after all you can't have the grown-ups disillusioned. Truth is, I don't think that I ever really did give up on Santa. I can't remember anything specific that my sister or I had as presents but we both would have had ample.

Boxing Day party was fun and Dad's treasure hunts had become the main event and were to continue for years to come. He bought presents for Mam, Alma and me, and never smoked again for the rest of his life. The only other memory I have of this Christmas is happiness and security.

Events during 1946 continued:

4 May – First class cricket returns, having been suspended during the War.

20 May – House of Commons votes to nationalise coal mines in the UK

31 May – London Heathrow Airport opened fully for civilian use.

1 June – Television licence introduced.

7 June – Television broadcasting by the BBC, suspended during World War II, resumes.

8 June – A victory parade is held in London to celebrate the end of World War II.

27 June – Government imposes bread rationing.

July – Homeless families squat in a former Army camp at Scunthorpe.

August – Arthur Homer, a member of the Communist Party, becomes General Secretary of the National Union of Mineworkers.

August – Finance Act receives Royal Assent, including the establishment of the National Land Fund to secure culturally significant property for the nation as a memorial to the dead of World War II.

6 Aug – Family allowance introduced, a cash benefit paid to mothers. – Free milk (1/3 pint daily) provided in UK state schools to all pupils under the age of 18.

31 Aug – League football returns, having been suspended during World War II.

September – November – "Britain Can Make It" exhibition at the Victoria and Albert Museum in London, produced by the Council of Industrial Design and the Board of Trade to show off good domestic and industrial design.

8 Sep – Mass squat by homeless families of the Ivanhoe Hotel and other empty properties in London organised by the Communist Party.

15 Sep – Bomber Harris retires.

15 Sep – Wilfred Pickles (*Have A Go*) first broadcast.

7 Oct – The BBC Light Programme transmits the first episode of the daily radio programme *Woman's Hour* which will still be running more than sixty-five years later.

17 Nov – Eight British Army servicemen are killed in Jerusalem by Jewish terrorists.

17 Nov – Tony Benn is elected as Treasurer of the Oxford Union.

26 Dec – David Leam's film of *Great Expectations* released.

Incidental items:

- Cinema going reaches an all time peak.

- Fred Pontin opens the first Pontins holiday camp, at Brean Sands, Burnham-on-Sea, Somerset.

- The Bush DAC90 bakelite radio introduced. It becomes the bestselling model for some years.

I think we had two weeks off school at Christmas. Dad only got two days, Christmas Day and Boxing Day, like most workers. New Year's Day was just another day, unless you were in Scotland or Scottish.

The Ballingers, a large rough family that lived over the road from us, had an eldest son who was still in the army and on leave over the New Year and, because he was in the *Black Watch*, they had a bit of a hooley on New

Year's Eve. He was quite tall, and I thought that he looked so smart in his "No. 1" Black Watch Dress complete with kilt. It looked a bit odd when he stepped out of the front door of that mad house, and then he would smartly walk around the town. It was a mad house, a noisy, happy, great bunch of kids.

It was just into 1947 and I was back at school and into my last year at junior school. The curriculum was the same, but focussing on all my worst subjects: reading, writing and maths. Everyone kept on about the Eleven Plus. Mam wanted me to go to the Tech School and become a draftsman, but not the Grammar School, as I was creative (No sweat there then). So, I would just knuckle down and do my best. Thought: I might just click in this year.

After school I would play outside for a couple of hours or round at someone's house, but it was so cold that year and I liked to get home in time for *Dick Barton, Special Agent* on the wireless at 6:45 every evening Monday to Friday. I was not allowed out again after this because my time limit was 7pm. *Dick Barton* did not finish until 7:15, and it was then cold and dark outside. We would always have a nice fire going in the living room and Mam would be doing something interesting, like embroidery, knitting or darning, so I used to muck in and was quite good at darning and embroidery.

My Dad said, 'Don't be shy about it,' as he had seen me hide my embroidery when my mates had called for me and told me how good some Army blokes were with a needle and thread. He showed me how to use a mushroom, a smooth piece of wood shaped like a mushroom that you would push into a sock or the like to hold a hole in its shape or position. Then you would darn the hole with a needle and wool or thread in a plaited "over and under" weaving fashion. He said mockingly, 'Every soldier gets issued with his own housewife.'

'Really?' I said, knowing that one of his funnies was about to emerge; then silence - followed by Mam taking over like a double act to explain the roll up holdall containing DIY cleaning, shaving, boot brushes, button stick, darning and sewing, tooth brush, etc. and officially called a housewife.

I had to smile a few years later when I did join the Army. I was being moved along this very long counter in the midst of a row of other young men in civilian clothes. As we were being frog-marched along, there were soldiers on the other side of the counter set out at intervals. Each one of them is slapping one item of equipment from the shelves behind him on the counter, whilst shouting out what it was, to which another soldier on our side would repeat what he shouted and tick it on his list. You would have to pick up the item on the move and get to the next soldier who was already banging the next item on the counter. You had to put all of these items into a large kit bag, which was your first item. Then, toward the end when you thought that you couldn't carry any more, let alone put it in your kit bag, the next squaddie shouted 'One housewife, for the use of.'

I said back to him, 'Just what I need right now.'

He laughed back. – it was called getting kitted out at the QM stores. A lot of young men didn't like being treated that way, but I thought it was great fun - and if you took it too seriously, you were dead.

Back home in '47, I even had a go at knitting, but I used to pull it too tight or too loose. When I tried "knit one, purl one, slip a stitch" it was a bit much for me and knew that I would not be world champion, so gave up. Alma was quite good, but sitting in, hearing the clicking of the knitting needles whilst listening to the wireless could be irritating. I used to look at Alma; she would be knitting, listening to the wireless and reading a book all at the same time. I could never do more than half a thing at once.

I suppose the street gang and I were in hibernation during those long, cold, dark nights. The wireless was getting more popular and varied after the war with some good plays and stories. I loved the wireless on with the music and people's different accents. News readers, announcers and presenters always had to speak with perfect diction. Even in a British movie a bank robber or a burglar would speak in clear English, unless it was a real character part like "Aarrr Jim lad". Swearing would be like, "I will get that ruddy blighter" or "Good heavens" - and such like.

So, in short, my life was good and I did like school and everything about dinner time. I ate everything and anything, except marmalade. We were into March now and my tenth birthday was approaching.

Events in the year 1947:

1 January – The government nationalises both the coal industry and Cable & Wireless Ltd in the UK.

2 January – British coins cease to include any silver content.

10 February – Major cuts in power supply due to shortages of fuel under severe winter conditions are imposed in England and Wales. – The BBC Television Service is temporarily suspended until 11 March.

20 February – Earl Mountbatten of Burma is appointed as the last Viceroy of India.

February – The coldest February in central England since records began in 1878 – average of - 1.9C (28.6F).

4 March – Treaty of Dunkirk (coming into effect 8 September) signed with France providing for mutual assistance in the event of attack.

Back in 1947, it is my birthday tomorrow and I will be ten years old, which completes a decade on this planet as a (sort of) human. It also marks the end of this book that I have called "Passing Clouds". It may get printed; it may not. Either way I have decided to step onto "Cloud Two" and continue my story and help to invent Rock & Roll all over again. Also the Eleven–Plus, finding a job and a girl, working hard, keeping fit and having the time of my life.

Thank you for reading.

Gordon Albert Arthur Kent

38089134R00216

Printed in Poland
by Amazon Fulfillment
Poland Sp. z o.o., Wrocław